Law School:
How to Get In,
Get Through,
and
Get Practicing

By Michael J. Reppas II, Esq.

Professionally Known As:
Michael J. Reppas II, B.A., J.D., LL.M., Esq.

PUBLISHED BY TRIMARK PRESS, INC., DEERFIELD BEACH, FLORIDA.

LIBRARY OF CONGRESS CATALOGING-IN-PUBLICATION DATA

LAW SCHOOL: HOW TO GET IN, GET THROUGH, AND GET PRACTICING
MICHAEL J. REPPAS II.

P. CM.

ISBN: 978-1-943401-45-1
LIBRARY OF CONGRESS CONTROL NUMBER: 2018947557
G18
10 9 8 7 6 5 4 3 2 1
FIRST EDITION
PRINTED AND BOUND IN THE UNITED STATES OF AMERICA

trimarkpress

A PUBLICATION OF TRIMARK PRESS, INC.
368 SOUTH MILITARY TRAIL
DEERFIELD BEACH, FL 33442
800.889.0693

DEDICATION

I would like to thank my first editor, Jessica Shraybman, for her interest and skill in getting my first draft ready to go while she was still in Law School. She is practicing law today, by the way, and doing very well thanks in large part to her reading this book – ha, ha.

I would also like to thank a few friends for their interest, support and comments on certain sections of this book, to wit: Bob Robes, Esq. and one other attorney who wishes to remain anonymous for fear of being sued by a completely made up character in this book whose made up name is "Liz" (read the book and find out why). I also would like to thank Lorie Greenspan, Barry Chesler and the team at TriMark Press for their excellent attention, editing and advice. It was a joy working with you.

I would be doing a disservice to the universe if I failed to thank my dear friend Kostas Vaxavaneris for his unending support of all of my artistic endeavors and for this fantastic book cover. He is a terribly talented artist and I am very thankful for his willingness to go the extra mile, every time, to make things "just right."

Finally, special thanks go out to my biggest fans: Anastasia, Michael, George and Zoe – without whom I would not care to exist.

Table of Contents

INTRODUCTION

The goal of this book is to take you from point "A" to point "B." Point "A" is that time in your life when you decided you wanted to go to law school. Point "B" is that time in your life when you have graduated from law school, have passed the bar, and have become a practicing attorney. It's a long road from "A" to "B." I expect this book will significantly help you prepare for that trip.

I wrote the draft of this book while I was actually in law school. I wrote it as sort of a diary. I kept record of significant events, classes and classmate experiences, and most particularly, significant moments that marked my change from "regular guy" to "attorney." I had a single purpose for doing this. I wanted to write a law school guide book for the prospective 21st century lawyer. More than just an autobiography of my law school experience, I wanted to write a book that would actually help people get into law school, get through it, and become attorneys.

I originally planned to edit and revise my "diary" after ten years of practicing law.[1] I wanted to wait all that time so that when I edited those writings I would be able to comment and elaborate on those experiences from the perspective of a seasoned attorney, not a recent graduate. Again, the goal was to create something much more than just a law school autobiography.

I wanted to write this book because, unlike the majority of

---

1 It actually took me closer to twenty.

my classmates, I did not have the luxury of having anyone guide me through law school. No one helped me prepare for the law school entrance exam or advised me on what to write in the application forms. No help in deciding which schools to apply to, or anything about financial aid or student loans. Sadly, I had no real information that would have helped me prepare for the journey I was about to undertake.

As a result, I had no help in understanding how to get into law school or, once there, what to do to succeed. I knew nothing and my road from "A" to "B" was a very difficult one. It was full of bad decisions, missed opportunities, unnecessary stops and avoidable roadblocks. Most of these were the direct result of having no guide to help me navigate.

The purpose of this book, therefore, is to give you the guidance I did not have. For this book to be the "person" who helps you. To give you advice on how to get into law school, how to get through law school, and how to get practicing as a lawyer.

This book is your mentor on the journey from "A" to "B."

I hope you find my "diary" an easy, enjoyable read that gives you insight into what law school is like. The excerpts included were selectively chosen. You will read anecdotes of some of my trials and tribulations and also find detailed summaries of each class I took.

After reading this book, you should be able to walk into school on the first day actually having a clue as to what is going on. This book will help you anticipate what will happen throughout your three years, and may even help you get better grades. In this regard alone it may be considered a practical guide, and may prove to be an invaluable addition to your bookshelf.

Good luck!

1

YOUR FIRST LESSON: HEARSAY

So, what is "hearsay?" Let's start with a definition:

HEARSAY hear'say'\ n —s often attrib {fr. the phrase hear- say]

1: something heard from another: REPORT

2: HEARSAY AS EVIDENCE: a legal concept evolved over hundreds of years in thousands of cases in the civil law tradition, constantly being redefined by teams of lawyers attempting to advance their client's cause at the expense of others.

3. SUGGESTED READINGS: any of a thousand long, boring and confusing books (many written in Old English) or "Law School: How To Get In, Get Through and Get Practicing" ©2018 by Michael J. Reppas II, Esq. 2

---

2 A shameless plug, I know.

The original title of this book was "It's All Hearsay!" Clever, but not Google friendly. While in law school, however, I thought it was important to start this book with a discussion of that term. It was my first legal epiphany. It was the first time I really understood a legal concept.

Throughout this book I will explain the law not as if I am speaking to an attorney, but rather as if I am teaching it to you for the first time — just as I learned it.

And hearsay is a great place to start. It is a legal rule which prohibits a witness from testifying about a statement made by someone else, outside of court, which is being used in court to prove the the statement is true. The actual definition you'll see in the text book is generally something like, "a declarant's out-of-court statement, used in court, to prove the truth of the matter asserted."

What does that even mean?! Settle down... I'll explain by using an example.

Let's say Peter is on trial for stealing Mary's Six Box CD Platinum COLLECTOR'S EDITION of J.Lo's Greatest Hits. Ignore the fact that J.Lo could never have a single Greatest Hits CD, let alone six. Just pretend it's true.

Now, at the trial, Mary's attorney calls Paul to the stand to testify.

What you don't know is that Peter, Paul and Mary go way back. Paul knows how much Peter loves J.Lo, and how jealous he was that Mary got the only greatest hits package that was ever made.[3] While Paul is on the stand sharing/relaying/testifying as to what he knows, he cannot say that "Peter told me he stole Mary's

---

3 Even JLo herself didn't get a copy.

J.Lo CDs." He can say that Peter's room is covered with posters of the great film star and musician, that he has 26 bottles of her perfume, "Love and Light" (that he intends on giving to "just the right girl") or that he has a photo album full of her concert photos and ticket stubs. But he cannot say that Peter admitted to him that he stole the CDs.

Why can't he say this? Because it's all hearsay!

If Paul could say "Peter told me he stole Mary's J.Lo CDs," the mere uttering of this statement would sound like proof to a jury that it was proof that Peter stole the discs. Remember that it is just a statement, not hard evidence. His statement is nothing tangible. If the judge let in that statement without any other evidence, would it be fair? Would it be enough to prove Mary's case and let her win?

If that statement were let in, then what would happen if it turned out that Paul made up the whole thing up because Mary promised she would finally sleep with him if he lied for her in court?[4] This is precisely why the hearsay rule was invented. Since Paul's testimony includes an out-of-court statement, which is being used to prove that Peter actually stole the discs, it is inadmissible evidence. Upon hearing Paul utter these words, any decent lawyer would immediately pipe up in the courtroom with a loud:

> *"Objection! Your Honor, that is inadmissible hearsay testimony that I ask be stricken from the record and I further ask that the jury be instructed to disregard same."*

---

4. Turns out Mary always hated Peter and had been waiting patiently for years for the opportunity to put him behind bars. She figured sleeping with Paul was a small price to pay for this sweet revenge.

The bottom line is if you want to know what Peter said you have to ask Peter, not Paul. Got it? Good.

The colloquial definition of "hearsay" usually includes the synonym "rumor." If you combine the legal and normal definitions you can see another reason that I had this as my original title. If anyone reading this book happens to have gone with me to law school, he or she may think they are one of the characters described somewhere in these pages. However, they are mistaken, because "It's All Hearsay!" Thus, if you think that the lower moron described on page 127 is actually you, then you're wrong (well... you're probably right, but I doubt you'd want to admit it to anyone).

...that was your appetizer, now let's get to the main course.

Since you are reading this book, you probably are considering going to law school and want to find out what it is like before you get there. Since that is the case, I have one question for you: Do you have the guts to do it? Not just the brains, but the guts?

I ask this for one simple reason. To get through law school, you will have to sweat for hours upon hours upon hours for days, weeks, months and years to graduate. Then you'll have to sweat a few hundred more hours to pass the Bar. And you better make sure that you pass on the first try, because nothing is more embarrassing and difficult to deal with than graduating with your Juris Doctor degree (your "J.D."), but not being able to practice. You have to get to Point "B."

Becoming an attorney is very difficult. Unless you are a genius, you must understand that you will have to spend most of your time (sorry, but that includes nights and weekends as well) studying. Don't get me wrong, there are indeed times when you can slack, however, it can't be your routine. If it is, especially in your first year, then you don't stand much of a chance of finishing.

2

Not An Island Vacation

Law school is a three-year tour of Hell. It's almost like being stranded on a deserted island. My use of the word "stranded" is very intentional. There are only a very, very few number of things you will be able to do on this island and only two places to go: home and school. During law school, especially your first year, every day will be the exact same monotony as the day before and the day after:

> Wake . . . study. . . eat. . . study. . . go to class
>
> Break . . . study. . . class. . . study really fast
>
> Eat. . . study. . . sleep. .. then the day has passed

Very quickly upon your arrival at law school you will feel "stranded." You will instantly realize that your deserted island extends only so far as the drive from your apartment to school. Nothing else will exist in your tiny new world. You will lose touch with current events, your favorite TV shows, your friends and loved ones, and virtually anything and everything that goes on in the world outside your island.

Your law school experience will include daily interaction with other inhabitants who have come to the same island from all across the country. Learning to deal with these people will be just as taxing on your constitution as will be studying for your classes.

In law school you will generally find that the number of students is small. One consequence of that small size is that everyone will know everyone else's business. Very well. Very quickly. You will see the same people day after day, over and over. It's almost like high school. Drama and all.

And just like high school, you will meet a handful of well-intentioned fellow law students with whom you may develop a friendship. There will also be a few rich kids, a few ex-jocks, bookworms, and probably a few dentists and doctors looking to change careers. Without question, however, you will definitely find a team of professors with the collective goodwill of all the former disgruntled employees of the United States Post Office.

You may get lucky and have a model-esque peer at whom to gawk, but for the most part you will find the island inhabitants to be a lot of energy drink/caffeine overdosed or otherwise crazed students running all over the place, freaking out over assignments and their futile attempts to get "outlines" from other students (I'll explain "outlines" later). What you need to know now is that these individuals will annoy the Hell out of you because they never stop. For three straight years they never stop. Be prepared.

If that wasn't enough, what makes law school even more difficult is that you have to study like mad for what seems like twen-

3

THREE TYPES OF LAW STUDENTS

There are basically three types of law students.

The first group I call the "Devoted Few." These students do nothing except eat and breathe the law. For them law school is a new religion, and they study the texts books like they are holy parchments. These individuals read and brief every case assigned, constantly update their outlines for every class, never fall behind in their work, participate in every class, are known by their first names by the professors (after the first two classes), and spend all their free-time doing more work. These individuals usually do the best in school. Unless, of course, they are major over-achievers. In that case they'll end up finishing in the middle of the class with fifty ulcers and a major addiction to antacids... amongst other things.

The second group I call the "Slackers." These individuals do the very least amount of work they think they can get away with, generally relax and enjoy their weekends, and almost without exception, are kicked out of school by the end of their first year.

As with everything in life, there are of course exceptions. Some slackers do manage to graduate, pass the bar, and have successful careers. These individuals are the great under-achievers who treat law school like the game it is and who live by the slogan "C = JD." These slackers understand that law school teaches you only how to "think like a lawyer." They know school doesn't teach them how to pass the Bar exam, how to practice law, or how to make money. For this reason, slackers are only willing to do the bare minimum they feel will get them a "C" in every class. They figure they'll get their JD and be on their way. Most people believe that these are the most vile and worthless people in law school. Others call them the most intelligent. I'm not one to judge, but I can tell you that one slacker I knew is now a judge, and another never passed the Bar. So I guess you never really know.

Finally, there is a third, intermediary group. I refer to this group in the singular as: "Your Average Law Student." Your Average Law Student is the one who slides back and forth between the worlds of the "Devoted" and the "Slackers." These individuals aspire to work as hard as the first group, but are sometimes pulled away from their celibate study into occasional relaxing weekends, Monday Night Football, and a general desire to have some kind of social life. Slacking can be great, but remember, law school costs most students about $75,000 a year.[5] That's a lot to pay to do nothing. So, in my humble opinion, slacking does not pay.

---

5. For tuition, books, supplies, and living expenses.

ty-four hours a day, seven days a week, for three solid years. The kicker is that you will have to deal with professors who teach by the Socratic Method of Intimidation and Interrogation, as well as a ton of wild-idiot students who have an opinion about everything and who fail to realize that nobody wants to hear them. You will interact with these people virtually every day for three years.

Law school is rough on many levels.

4

WHAT KIND OF LAW STUDENT WAS I ?

I was somewhere between "devoted" and "your average law student." Going into law school, I was 100% certain that I was going to specialize in Immigration and International Law so I was completely "devoted" to those classes. I wrote papers for those classes, read and briefed EVERY case (assigned and unassigned), and had incredibly detailed outlines. Thankfully the effort was reflected in the grades I received: top of the class, all across the board. I got awards for being the top student in several classes, made Law Review, and even got published.

In classes not "international" in nature or that otherwise did not interest me (like family and criminal law), I was more between the "Intermediary" group and the "Slackers." My grades reflected that as well. Let me make a comment here. I do not practice immigration law. In fact, at no point in my career have I ever practiced immigration law. I tell you this so that you understand that even if you go into law school with 100% certainty that you will practice criminal law (because of all the "Law & Order" episodes that you have memorized and acted out in front of the mirror), you still might end up doing something completely different. You might even find yourself not even practicing law at all.

5

How To Get Into Law School

I worked in a very prestigious law firm in my home town for a couple of years before I decided to apply to law school. Over that time, I learned a great deal about the relationship between the kings and the peasants, *i.e.*, the attorneys and the rest of the staff. Data entry clerks, like me, were at the bottom of the barrel. Janitors ranked higher because they were needed every now and then. Nobody actually needs a data entry clerk.

I realized after a very short time that if given a choice I would rather be a king than a peasant. The way the attorneys carried themselves, that swagger, was almost tangible. They were admired, respected, even worshiped. They drove the best cars, lived in mansions, and partied like rock stars (whom they of course represented). Essentially, they had the exact opposite life I did. At least that's how I saw it. I was the guy serving the drinks in the fancy restaurant rather than enjoying the dinner.

My mission was to become a king.

I began intentionally interacting with the firm's attorneys. I joined the firm's baseball and soccer teams and started interacting. After a while and to my great relief and surprise, I found that I was just as articulate as most of them and just as educated, minus the law degree. I came to realize that the only real difference was that they were attorneys and I wasn't. Also, they were rich and I wasn't, but that was for the same reason.

One night at home I was watching a rerun of *Star Trek: The Next Generation*. It was the episode where Picard gets "assimilated" by the Borg. I suddenly realized that I needed to be "assimilated" too. I needed to gain the "collective" knowledge of all the attorneys I worked for. I decided then and there that "resistance was futile." The only way for me to get there was to go to law school.

Now I just had to figure out how to do that.

Get Accepted to a Law School

Getting accepted to law school sounds much easier than it actually is. It can be a major pain. Even with the right qualifications. So how do you get in? For starters, you need to have a four-year undergrad degree and to have done well while getting it. Then you have to take the LSAT (pronounced as two words: "L - sat"). The LSAT is basically a standardized IQ test, not much different than the one you took to get into college, only a lot harder.

The two most important factors that law schools consider in new applicants are undergrad grade point averages and LSAT scores. Each school has its own minimum score requirements. For example, one law school may only consider applicants with a 3.3 GPA and 150 LSAT. Another school may only consider applicants with a 3.7 GPA and 170 LSAT. Because each school is different, what you'll need to get in will depend on the caliber of school to which you are applying and your particular scores. Obviously, the higher your scores, the better your chances to get in, to get scholarships, etc.

To get accepted into your top choice school, you may have to take the LSAT more than once (after an expensive prep course, of course). Best bet is to take the prep course before trying your luck on your own – a lesson I had to learn first hand.

Taking the LSAT a second time can benefit you significantly if you improve your score. Here's how: if you score a 145 on the first test and a 155 on the second, your LSAT score is reported as 150. Note however, that if the school you want to attend has a minimum of 155, you are out of luck… you should have taken the prep course the first time.

After all that, you have to get the right letters of recommendation. This was another reason I wanted to work at a law firm for some big-shot attorneys. Letters from college professors, priests/rabbis/ministers, and old bosses are good too.

You should avoid offering your letter writers too much "help." It's understandable that you want all your respectable attributes to be included, but don't be overly zealous. Rather than the letter saying, "He's a good boy that goes to church every Sunday, after he donates blood for the Veteran's Hospital and volunteers at the animal shelter," you may end up with, "He's a pushy, demanding know-it-all who thinks he is above everyone around him." While that might be true, it is not something you want in your recommendation letter. Be choosey when asking someone to write on your behalf, and stay on their good side ... at least until you get accepted.

Next, you have to write a "personal statement" and fill out the dreaded applications with all their stupid questions. For example: "What volunteer services have you performed in the last year that you feel have been of benefit to your community?" What a pain in the ass. All you want to say is "What the hell do you care? Why are you involving morality and altruism in this application form? For goodness sake I want to be an attorney, not a priest!" But you won't write that. You better not if you want to get in anyway. You must force out a politically correct response. Even though it really tells them nothing, you want to highlight your moral upbringing. This tells them that you are willing to play the game and that's what they want to hear.

Let me give you an example. What I submitted to the admissions offices and what I wanted to submit were two completely different things. I wanted to begin the personal statement by showing off one of my strongest talents: writing. I decided to compose a poem that would show the admissions people exactly how clever and talented I was. I ended up with two separate poems. I am including them here for you so that you might better understand the "right" and "wrong" ways to start your statement. The first one, the "wrong" way, is as follows:

<u>Revelations During the Composition</u>
<u>of Law School Applications</u>

The world is an oyster
Gimme a break and let me grab the pearl

Come on
I've busted my ass over the last few years
I deserve a shot at the rings

How to Get Into Law School

Just a shot
What do you say

Besides, if I fuck up don't forget
That I have to swallow that slimy oyster
Gross
Roll the bones baby

Gimme a break
Let me ravage your oyster

That poem came from my exasperation/frustration/irritation of having to jump over so many hurdles to get into law school. I liked this version even though it was a bit raw. For some reason though, I didn't think the admissions people would appreciate it as much as I did. Maybe a little too much truth in there?

Anyway, I worked hard and wrote the perfect suck-up sonnet. The poem below, the "right" way to start a personal statement, is untitled.

The law is a precise discipline that calls to devout students
As with a poem, you must submerge yourself in its essence and form
For there is no value in partial involvement
A disciple in either school would constantly strive for more

And shall we discuss their eloquence, how their wisdom is portrayed
Through a judge's Opinion and poet's Sonnet
Both deeply rooted in emotion, then sculpted by intelligence
Such are the accomplishments that mark human progress

Law is the culmination of man's ethics and good sense
It accurately displays the values of society
It urges civilization forward by reflecting benevolence
The law is the guideline to conscientious morality

If one is able to find meaning therein, and not lose sight of humanity
Then their achievement purpose and style have proven them worthy

Do you see the difference? The second poem is elegant, so-phisticated and meaningless all rolled into one. Perfect for a law school application! It emphasized my writing talent and my passion for law. At the same time, it kisses-up quite well. "Wisdom," "discipline," "intelligence," "ethics," "benevolence," "morality" … "human progress." All the concepts I wanted to get across in my own, personal way.

That was the introduction for my personal statement. You will have to find an angle to make your own point with style. Just keep in mind that you are "hoop-jumping." Give 'em what they want. Play the game.

After all your applications are out, you sit and wait. And wait. And wait. It will seem like a lifetime of waiting before you get any response. Note that this is a foreshadowing of how you will feel awaiting Bar results.

Hopefully you'll get into at least one school. If not, go back to the end of the line and start jumping from the beginning. If you do get into a school, CONGRATULATIONS! You now have my permission to read the rest of this book.

You may be lucky enough to get into more than one school. If so, you have to decide where you want to live for the next three years. If out of state, consider whether you want to stay in that place for the long haul. Where you go to school will likely determine where you'll end up practicing for the rest of your life. [6]

It's a big game, kids. A big game broken up into little parts. The first part, the Tryouts, is about getting into law school. Once you're in, you enter the next part: Spring Training. This is where you proceed to kill yourself for three years to prove to the coach that you're good enough to actually play. Finally you graduate. In this part you add a cool acronym to your name ("JD"), pass the Bar, and jump into the big game: "Life as an Attorney." [7] Hopefully, you'll end up in the major, not the minor league. Rest easy for now. That is an issue resolved on draft day.

You're not there yet.

Following the baseball analogy, I suppose if you win some really big cases you'll be inducted into the Hall of Fame and they'll make dramatic movies about your great courtroom skill. Now that's something to shoot for. Too bad Dustin Hoffman will be too old to play me. With my luck, they'd probably choose Daniel Radcliffe anyway.

Student Loans

One of the most important things to consider about law school, especially if you go to a private school as I did, is how much money it costs to attend. Tuition could run $50,000 a year. Living expenses will run at least $15,000 a year (give or take). Add a few grand for books and spending money and that's around $70,000 a year. If you don't come in with scholarship, or your folks don't have an extra $200,000 lying around, then you are going to need to take out student loans. Loans are usually easy to get unless you

6. Sorry to all the Alaskan law students out there.
7. That sounds like a good title for A/the sequel.

have a crappy credit history . . . like one of my buddies.

My buddy screwed up his credit when he was younger. He's still a pretty young guy so he hasn't had the chance to rebuild his credit score. He ended up not having enough money to cover his tuition and his housing costs. He got a loan through the school, which was enough to cover his tuition, but because of his poor credit, additional loans were denied. So he went to his parents.

Unfortunately, his folks did not have money to spare. Moreover, they refused to co-sign on any of his loans. They were probably worried how it would affect their credit. Either way, he didn't have money to cover housing and was facing the reality that he may not have a room come second semester. No shit. The housing department told him that unless he came up with the money by the time spring registration came around, he would not be allowed to register. He had four days.

The poor guy was freaking out. He busted his ass to get into law school, busted his ass to get the initial funds, and busted his ass to do well his first semester. Now he could lose it all because he didn't have enough money or credit. It really wasn't fair. Especially this close to exams.

A persistent guy, he kept after his folks, and kept bugging the shit out of the school's financial aid director. The four days passed, but his situation hadn't changed. The school, very surprisingly, allowed him to register and gave him an extra week to come up with the money – or at least get a loan approval.

Thankfully this story does have a happy ending. His father finally agreed to co-sign his loans. However, there was a condition. His father would keep the money, and only give it to him as needed. Not very trusting, but I don't know what he did to screw up his credit in the first place, so maybe the ubercaution was justified. I'm just glad he finally got the money and could stay in school. Man that was close.

So, the moral of the story: think hard about how you are going to finance your three-year education. You don't want to get into a situation where you invest all your time and energy getting to law school only to find out that you can't stay because you can't afford it. On the whole, most people can get the loans and go to school, so don't worry too much about it, but just remember that if you take out $200,000 in student loans, by the time you pay it back you would have spent over $300,000 . . . or some enormous, ridiculously burdensome amount.

So to quickly sum up here: your goal is to get through law school owing as little as humanly possible.

THE FIRST YEAR

6

Orientation

"**W**elcome to law school!" the thick voice victoriously declared. He stood behind the podium, brazing a large, toothy smile from one drooping ear to the other, his hands high in the air as if he had just won a marathon. The auditorium erupted with the sound of applause.

"Congratulations to each and every one of you!" he cheered. More applause. "You 125 have been selected from a pool of over 3,500 applicants for this year's class." More applause. "You are the creme de la creme; the stars! You are very special students who have proven yourselves worthy of studying law." The applause continued until the smile left his face. His tone then changed from that of a head coach at a high school pep rally to that of an uninspired funeral pastor.

"Stop applauding yourselves. The party is over. You are now entering the most grueling three years of academic study you could ever have imagined." He paused and he let the weight of this statement sink into the once excited, but now stunned crowd.

"Say goodbye to your husbands and wives, children, girl-friends, boyfriends, family, and friends. Say goodbye, because for the next three years you won't have any time to see them." You could hear a few muffled laughs of doubting fear, but the speaker refused to acknowledge them. Instead, he continued in that dull and depressing monotone as if his goal was to reemphasize the severity of our punishment. At this point any remnants of excitement we felt at our "welcoming party" slipped away.

"Say goodbye to your social life, say goodbye to everything, and say hello to the library." I wasn't sure if he was trying to make a joke, but he didn't smile. No one else did either. "Yes, One-L's," he continued, "you will all discover your new church in the library. You will worship in the library more than you think humanly possible. You will worship there and use Black's Law Dictionary as your Bible. This time will be a true test of your character. This time will fashion you into hard working, knowledgeable, and dedicated attorneys. This time will shape you into the professional you will be for the rest of your career. So forsake the life you knew yesterday, and prepare to embrace your new reality of devout study and sleep deprivation." The auditorium remained absolutely silent.

The law school Dean saw the petrified faces turn from pale to ghostly white and nodded in satisfaction. He was pleased with himself and his speech. He paused a few more seconds to soak in just a bit more of the sadness and shock. Then he broke the silence with a rather upbeat announcement. "I am pleased to tell you that you all have access to the campus counselor's office and to stress management courses. These will help you transition into your new lifestyles." The crowd's outrage grew by the second.

"Take my advice. Use these services," he continued. "This next year, your first semester especially, will make you work harder than you ever have in the past. Harder than you thought you ever could. You will have to work hard, because if you ever fall behind in a class –" he let this dangle in the air a moment – "well… let's just say that the amount of reading and briefing you'll have to do to catch up will be overwhelming. There is simply too much work assigned every day to allow for any extra time to do anything. So, if you fall behind, even a little, it will be virtually impossible to catch up. And you don't want to skip any material because every case you brief has been based upon the one you briefed before. Miss a brick and the building falls."

At this juncture, the Dean seemed a bit disappointed. He realized no one appreciated his good words of advice. They all seemed more upset than appreciative. He continued nonetheless. "Learning the law means building a courthouse in your head. Piece by piece, case by case, law by law, theory by theory. It ends with an understanding of why and how all the cases, laws and theories relate. But that understanding will not come anytime soon. It will take diligent work each and every day to ensure that you get the 'full picture.' But don't worry if for the first few weeks or so you have no idea what's going on. Keep at it. Keep studying night and day, and eventually it will all come to you. Some day when you are sitting in your church, the light of Heaven will shine upon you and you will say 'Yes , I see it … I finally see it!'" He raised his hands in a mock Hallelujah gesture.

This last acting exercise was made in an obvious attempt to elicit laughter. However, people did not react whatsoever. A few students in the front few rows shuffled in their seats and giggled nervously. Their laughs were quiet, but loud enough to let the Dean know his wit and wisdom weren't falling on deaf ears.

The Dean then laughed a jolly and hearty laugh like he was

now Santa Clause, trying to convince everyone of his good nature. Trying to convey the sense that he was our friend, not our warden. He smiled at the students in the first two rows as thanks for their attention, support and acknowledgment of his comic genius. He then continued with his deathly monotone.

"In this first semester you will brief so many cases that you will not even be able to remember when you last ate or were even hungry. But please... remember to eat." He paused at this dramatic draw he spun into a joke, almost as if he were expecting an "Applause Sign" to start flashing. This time no one laughed or even giggled – not even the suck-ups in the first row. He didn't seem bothered. He was on a roll and was going to keep the jokes coming.

"Please... remember to breathe." Again no laughter. "Remember to take care of yourselves. Exercise and try to maintain some sort of life outside of school, otherwise you will go crazy." He tried to leave on a high note and smiled at everyone warmly. Taking time to turn his head from corner to corner of the room. Taking time to make eye contact with those students courageous enough to look him in the eyes.

He scanned the entire room and seemed a little disappointed that no one was laughing at his hilarious ending. He exhaled in disappointment and without any real conviction stated: "Okay, that's it from me. Good luck everyone," and he quietly left the podium.

No one laughed. No one cheered. No one applauded. You don't act that way at a funeral and this was definitely a funeral. I looked around to judge the reaction of the crowd. It seemed there were only two people not crippled by shock and fear: yours truly and the guy sitting next to me. We had both been sarcastically snickering throughout the Dean's chilling speech, and were obviously not moved by the horror story/welcome speech.

I asked if he was scared by the Dean's apocalyptic predictions of our future. He responded with a quick "Yeah, and all we need now is a campfire and some marshmallows and it'll be just perfect!" He looked away before he could see me smile.

The "Red Scare" of the State Board of Examiners

"Congratulations on your acceptance into law school," the Demon in a red dress dully stated upon reaching the podium. Her underwhelmed tone made it immediately obvious she was not an eager or willing participant. Even from her first few words, it was clear she was bothered by us. Annoyed even.

She paused and slowly peered across the room with an edgy, almost disgusted visage. As I watched her, I felt she was the exact opposite of Helen of Troy, and I immediately wanted to go home to Ithaca.

She continued, "I am here to talk to you about the process of becoming a member of the Florida Bar Association. Our State has the highest bar standards in the United States. Some other states have only two or three pages of information that they require from their applicants. We have a much more detailed inquiry here. Our application is long. Very long and very intimate." Intimate? I thought to myself ... intimate?

"The Board will ask you questions that will make you feel completely naked," she said matter-of-factly. Was it just me or was she trying to tell us that we were about to get screwed? "We will ask you questions regarding every job you have ever held, every credit transaction you have ever made, every bank account you have ever opened, about any and every encounter with the police, about your educational background in detail, and about virtually every commercial entity you have had relationships with in the past."

Considering that the Demon's speech came at the heels of the Dean's warm welcome, the reaction of the students reflected a general sense that they had had enough doom and gloom for one morning. Also considering that this speaker was not our new Dean, or even a professor at the law school, the quiet and respectful response given to the Dean was not going to be repeated.

Within seconds, the hecklers began with muffled cries of "Jesus," "Come on," and "Give me a break!" She continued irrespective of the crowd's growing adversarial disposition. Perhaps inspired by the opposition, the tone of voice took on a more confrontational tone.

"We are the most thorough Bar Association in the country because we believe that the ethical character of prospective lawyers in our state is paramount. To be quite frank, we want the best attorneys we can possibly have so we diligently investigate all prospective attorneys. We do this to ensure that every future client you may have will be represented by a moral, competent, responsible, and honest attorney. And to that end you will be asked to voluntarily submit to us a detailed explanation of every major problem you have had in your life."

The hecklers broke out at this last statement. "What?!" "Are you serious?" She continued, ignoring them all. "You will have to come clean on your past. You will have to because our investigative team – made up of former FBI agents – will be verifying every statement you make." More disruption from the hecklers.

"We will do a complete search into everything about you. We will run computer searches through every criminal, credit, and school system you have interacted with." As if on cue, the hecklers reacted with hostile outbursts. Their numbers were growing and the protest decibel level was rising.

The Demon didn't miss a beat. "And we will compare your answers with every application you ever completed for other law schools – no matter how many schools you applied to – to ensure that your answers were consistent on each application. If you omitted any information on one application, or indeed lied on that application, we will want to know why." Did they have the resources to pull this off? I wondered.

At this point everyone became a heckler and a few students even began to yell. At this, she raised her voice, got closer to the microphone and continued louder than ever – almost shouting. "It is advisable that if any of you gave incorrect information to the admissions office at this law school, that you should take it upon yourselves to write a written letter of apology to the Dean and explain to him what information was incorrect and how so. You should also tell him why you gave false information. You should be prepared to be dismissed if, in light of that information, you are deemed to be unqualified to be a member of this law school class."

Someone in the back of the auditorium yelled out: "You guys are the Gestapo!" There were a few nervous laughs, but all eyes and ears quickly returned to the podium. The Demon, the moral goddess of the Bar Association, stood her ground and stared into the crowd attempting to make eye contact with the student who called her a Nazi. She attempted to regain control and reassert her dominance. In support, the Dean rose to his feet, faced the crowd and motioned for them to calm and quiet down.

After the crowd settled, the Dean retook his seat and the Demon continued. "If you have a problem in your past, say an arrest or a conviction for an open container violation as an undergrad, a D.U.I., a D.W.I., traffic violations..." she took a deep breath and continued. "If you ever declared bankruptcy, or defaulted on a loan, or had some credit problems, or didn't declare some income from working under the table, we will want to know about that. If you were ever suspended or expelled from school, we will want to know why. And believe me, we will find out about all of these indiscretions so it's best to disclose everything up front." Silence.

"These problems in your past do not necessarily mean you will not be admitted to the Bar. I address them here for you so that you understand that it is in your best interest to disclose everything to us, and to suggest that you clean up any loose ends that may be dangling around your neck. Quickly. Show the Board that you are honest and have become a moral and upstanding citizen." The auditorium returned to chaos.

Hands flew into the air seeking to be called upon. Heated voices questioned the justice in the Board's activities. Some kids even challenged the morality of the speaker herself. One guy, not waiting to be called upon, blared out "How can we trust the members of the Board to be honest in their investigations?" It was loud enough that the Demon stopped and answered him.

"The Board members are all highly moral people who are, by the way, volunteers, and only seek to ensure the highest level of truth and integrity in the legal profession."

"Yeah right," the student retorted.

"Don't worry," the Demon calmly stated, "everything they discover and discuss with you will remain confidential."

The student continued, "Sure, but who are they accountable to... who do they answer to?" She did not immediately respond, but ultimately restated her previous statement that the Board members "were honest and trustworthy." Then the floodgates opened and questions poured over her. The remaining minutes of her speech were, to say the least, intense.

Do you remember the history of Joe McCarthy? He was the guy in the 1950s who went around accusing everyone of being a Communist. Remember? Think history class... ninth grade. It was the time when the big "Red Scare" poured across our country. The time when everyone's past was being thrown at them like daggers. People, good people, were banished from society if they were deemed a "Communist" – even though most of those stone throwers didn't even know what a Communist really was.

This was the time in our history when people were condemned and labeled traitors for political reasons. Condemned just for being the friend of a so-called "Communist"... or for having a discussion at a bar one night with a stranger who turned out to be a Communist for one week while in college, or for accidentally bumping into one at a bus stop. This was a sad time in our history. A time when the Cold War was getting hot. We were being indoctrinated to hate the Soviets, and our Greatest American Hero and Senator, Joe McCarthy, was the spokesman for this ignorant movement. One might analogize the Demon in the red dress to good 'ol Joe, and allege that the Board of Bar Examiners was perpetrating its own Red Scare.

If you are a prospective One-L and are especially concerned

with how the Bar Examiners are going to treat you because of a particular skeleton in your past, I suggest that you find out your state Board's disposition before you start law school. If you can't get to Point "B," don't start the journey.

The Purpose of the First Year of Law School

Orientation will be your introduction to law school horror stories, which are all true. You get no sleep, have no social life, and do nothing but study 24/7/365 for three years. Incredible academic challenges. Huge stress. Major competition. You may ask, "But why?"

After completing Orientation and having several conversations with professors and upperclassmen, I thought I had figured it out. Now, twenty years after passing the Bar, I can tell you that I still agree with my first impression. It's a simple answer but requires a long explanation.

The simple answer is that your law school wants you to succeed. They want you to be a competent and successful attorney. Why? Don't they only care about the incredibly expensive tuition? Yes, that's a fair observation, but they also need as many successful alumni as possible to gain credibility. You want to go to their law school because Mike Reppas or some other superstar went there. You get my point. They look good if you do well. The better you are as a practicing attorney, the better the school becomes.

Res ipsa loquitur (look it up). They want to be able to brag that they were the direct and proximate cause of your success. In other words, they want to ride your coattails. You with me?

So why does your experience need to be a three-year trip to Hell? The stock answer is because that is how long it takes to get you to "think like a lawyer." This means they will force you to think like an attorney from Day One. They want you to figure it out A.S.A.P., sink or swim. If you don't, you're out. It is that simple.

In your first year, expect to brief hundreds of cases, be called upon and humiliated in front of your peers (and that cute girl you were trying to impress), be thrown out of class for lack of full preparation or being ten seconds late. Schools claim you are treated this way to prepare you for attorney-hood. When you start practicing you will be used to the hyper-confrontational, super-intense pressure chamber that is the American courtroom.

In theory that's all fine and dandy, but it is a different thing entirely when you're being mercilessly grilled by a professor. That, as they say, is when the men are separated from the boys. When it happens to you, you learn that the BBQ is a very lonely place. Lonely because you are left to roast on your own. You won't get any assistance from peers because they want to avoid the confrontation/roast and save themselves. In class, there are no "Heroes" or "White Knights." If anyone does try to be a Good Samaritan, he or she will quickly feel the heat from the fire pit.

You'll find that professors quite often turn on the "Hero" to frighten others from raising their hands. And believe me, they want this fear. Pure, unwavering, hand-shaking fear. Volunteering is for fools or idiots who never seem to appreciate the absolute thrashing they take every time they open their mouths.

The Purpose of the First Year of Law School

Professors justify the excessive hardship with the usual "to make you a good attorney" rhetoric. They believe legal reasoning is like hand-solved long-division equations. You must show your work to demonstrate your logic/understanding. They are training you to make the most persuasive legal arguments that can be made. After your training, you'll have the ability to act on your feet, to think quickly and intelligently and to be, you guessed it: fearless and persuasive!

It's a logical game that requires you to deconstruct then reconstruct your case. It is a method of teaching that forces you to argue why some facts are more important than others, and thus, why some cases are more applicable than others. When in court, the judge won't give you multiple choice questions. You will have to convince the judge which law he should apply in deciding your case. That's your job: convince the judge; convince the jury.

You will do this by identifying the facts, finding case law with similar facts (a process not so mysteriously called "legal research"), and by developing your legal argument therefrom. Your argument will include an analysis and application of previous court decisions (known as "precedents"), will be framed on those precedents, and will argue which precedent should or should not be used to determine the verdict at bar.

Law school is not about learning an objective set of rules. You don't show up and start memorizing all the laws as they are currently written. Rather, law school is a method of teaching you how to discover and apply legal rules to your case. As one wise professor told me, "the law is whatever the most persuasive advocate tells you it is. The facts are the key; make the facts work for you."

The purpose is to give you the ability to take any type of case and know how to identify the relevant facts, find all the precedents, know what to argue, and know how to win. "Thinking like an attorney" is not a meaningless cliché. In fact, it is exactly the skill you take away from your three years.[8]

Let's face it – our society values winners. Someday, when you're at Point "B," you will have clients paying you tens of thousands of dollars to win their case. Not to come in second. You need to win. And this is not just for the paying clients. Those of you that want to become attorneys to make a difference in the world, to help some charity or cause or person in need, you need to be winners as well. A bad advocate can harm a good cause.

Everybody wants to win, and you are no exception. That's why you want to go to law school. You want to win that big case in court. You want to walk in front of the jury and tell them why your client should win. You want to be the big shot. Come on ... admit it! I know I do. I want to win all my cases. I want to win every motion, every hearing, and every trial. I enjoy the challenge. I enjoy the battle with opposing counsel. I enjoy judges and juries. I enjoy the excitement of it all. I am not a TV actor. I am real and so are my clients.

Speaking of actors, there is a theory which states that trial attorneys are all failed actors. This may actually be true, but if we are to analogize law school and acting school, the better comparison would be with improv. As mentioned earlier, unlike actors reciting scripts verbatim, trial attorneys do not read prepared lines.

We are forced to make them up as we go and respond quickly and authoritatively to every hurdle put in our way.

---

8 Along with your diploma, of course ... and a million dollars in student loans!

The Purpose of the First Year of Law School

One myth many people have about attorneys is that they know every law that was ever written. Another is that your three years in school are spent memorizing all those laws. Both are major misconceptions.

There are literally thousands upon thousands of rules, precedents, and different types of laws. No matter how brilliant you may be, you could never memorize them all. That's why law school is not about memorizing the law, it's about teaching you how to find and apply the laws you need to win your case. They teach you how to be an "analytical thinker," and you will learn how to recognize the essential facts a new client provides you and how to find and argue the right law to win that case. That way, when you're at Point "B," and a prospective client comes into your office and tells you his story, you can determine the critical facts, do your legal research, and be able to tell that client exactly why, or why not, he has a case.

That, my friends, is "thinking like an attorney," and that is what you will learn in law school.

8

How To Get A Feel Of What You'll Be Doing Your First Semester at Law School

Legal research and creative argument are keys to being an effective advocate. Law school teaches you how to find and argue the "right" law by, you guessed it: legal research and creative argument. The goal of research is to find favorable precedent to support the claims or defenses of your client, while simultaneously identifying and explaining away the counter arguments. You use cases with similar facts as yours to convince the court that it should apply the same law as the other court did in the case you are using. Obviously, you don't want to argue a case with similar facts as yours where the court ruled against your side.[9] You want

---

9 VOICE FROM THE FUTURE: This is not as simple as it sounds. As you will note farther down the road when you are a practicing attorney, you are an "Officer of the Court," and are ethically required to disclose a "bad precedent" to the court – even if your opponent fails to do so. Crazy, right? No one would actually do this, right? Let me get this straight, you find the perfect case for your opponent, the case that guarantees that they win and you lose, but your opponent misses it, and you are supposed to disclose that case to the Judge? Really? Does anyone actually do that? Well that last one is a rhetorical question because I don't know any attorney who would intentionally throw their client (and their client's case) under the bus by doing the other guy's work. I doubt such an attorney would have a lot of clients if he did. It is an ethical obligation to disclose the information though, so it's a bit of a Catch-22 here. How would you proceed?

to use a case with similar facts that have a result which favors your client.

Here's what you want to say: "Judge, I want a million dollars because the plaintiff in my precedent case got a million dollars and the facts are the same, so my client deserves the same treatment under the law."

To illustrate, let's say your client got drunk, dressed-up like a Christmas Elf (in the middle of June) and got busted for possession of a controlled substance and public indecency. He was apprehended in front of the courthouse while tap dancing, singing "Superfreak" very loudly, and de-robing. Good client you got there. [10]

You start your legal research by finding a case that tells you what constitutes "possession." Get the details from the case law, pull the statutes (the state or federal laws made by your legislature on the subject), and compare those details with the facts in your client's case. Maybe carrying less than 1 ounce of the drug calls for a fine rather than incarceration; maybe you learn something that helps you or your client better understand what exactly you are up against and what you might be able to get away with. After you finish researching "possession," do the same thing with "public indecency." And keep going.

Legal research is not about hoping and praying that somewhere, sometime, some other lush, cross-dressing, pot-head got away with "carrying" while dressed as a fairy. [11] It's about finding something relevant which you can apply to your case. Maybe in this case you'll find precedents that discuss freedom of speech,

---

10 **ANOTHER VOICE FROM THE FUTURE:** in real life if you do get such a client I offer you one piece of advice: get paid up front.
11 Though... considering our society you may just find such a case.

freedom of expression, or some other law that you can use to explain away why your client is not a lunatic and does not deserve to be locked up. Got it? That is how you do it. Legal research and creative argument.

In your first semester, you will be assigned a plethora of cases to read for each class. You will have to "brief" each case. Briefs are basically case summaries including the important points, the law applied, and the outcome. Your briefs, combined with your notes form your "outline," become your study guide for the class. As some put it- your Bible. You will endeavor to memorize your outlines during finals week.[12] Thus, your briefs, even from Day One, are very important.

Understand that the cases you read are the **judge's written opinions** of what happened in that particular case – factually and legally. Each case/opinion is a story about X suing Y for something and how and why the court decided the way it did.

After briefing a case, you will be able to quickly identify what issues of law the court was deciding, what was the final decision, and why the court (another way to refer to the judge is "the Court," by the way) decided the way it did. As previously noted, these decisions are collectively called "case law," more commonly referred to as "precedents."

To give you another head start, let me show you how to brief a case. So this is not too overwhelming, I am going to start out with a simple form. You will learn to detail and improve as you develop your briefing skills.

First write down the name of the case, the court that made the decision, and the year of the decision (*e.g.*, Franklin v. Frank-

---

12 We'll go into far more detail regarding Outlines later.

lin, Florida Supreme Court, 1980). Then make a section detailing the facts of the case – it's history; you know... the story. **FACTS:** Billy and Bobby were childhood friends and shared everything. On Jan. 24, Bobby stole one of Billy's favorite baseball cards from his locker (if you want to be specific you can say it was a Barry Bonds card); Billy ran over Bobby with his moped and took back the card from his mangled, bloody hand, and then sped home with a smile on his face.

Next, determine the "issue," *i.e.*, what question the court was being asked to decide. Our brief might look like this: "**ISSUE:** Whether a kid may run over another kid with his moped if the 'victim' first stole one of his baseball cards."

You're doing great kids, stay with me.

The next section of your brief explains how the court decided the case. **HOLDING**: Assaulting someone for stealing a Barry Bonds baseball card is against the law.

Lastly, you detail why the court ruled that way it did. **REASONING**: assaulting someone for stealing a Barry Bonds baseball card is against the law even though Barry Bonds baseball cards have no value.

Sounds simple, right? Well it ain't. It may take 30 minutes to an hour to brief a ten-page case. The time depends on how many times you have to read it. Let's say you have to brief 50 cases a week for each of your five classes. Run your calculation and tell me how much sleep deprivation that comes out to.

<u>Attention all overachievers</u>: If you want to actually try and brief some cases BEFORE you go to law school, here is a helpful book: *The Legal Writing Handbook, Research, Analysis, and Writing*, written by: Oates, Enquist, and Kunsch. It will give you a

lot more detail which you'll likely need anyway. Understand that as you progress, your style will change to fit your needs. That's okay; that's normal; that's good. You have to build your home before you arrange the furniture.

If you want to take this pre-law school prep course to the next level, go buy a casebook. You choose the subject: Torts, Contracts, or Criminal Law, but not Civil Procedure (I'll tell you why later, but suffice it to say this class is not very easy to understand). Where do you get these books? Your neighborhood academic bookstore, of course. I would go there and ask one of the salespeople where the first-year law student books are, and pick out a subject you might like. Look around. See how expensive everything is. See how sad and nervous the law students are who are shopping there. Get depressed. Rethink your career plans.

Also get a copy of a corresponding "Case Notes®" for that book. Case Notes provide you with sample briefs done by "professionals" for each of the cases found in the casebook.[13] Most law schools tell you never to buy commercial outlines, but they are hypocrites because they sell them in their own bookstores and make big bucks off of them. They tell you that if you buy these outlines then you will never learn how to brief a case correctly. I say go ahead and get them. They show you how the big guns briefed the case, and, invariably, will show you what you missed in your own brief. However, to use them effectively, read and brief the case on your own FIRST, then compare your brief with the Case Notes.

Another tip: even if it's a lot cheaper, don't buy a used book covered with a previous student's notes. It will not help you to see

---

13 FYI: "Case Notes"® is a registered trademark for a series of commercial outlines sold in every law school.

what another student thought was important. He/she may have been a genius or an idiot – why risk it? Get a new book and fill it out for yourself.

Another FYI: expect to pay about $250 for these two books. No one ever said law school was cheap.

When you are starting out and realize how badly you are doing, don't get discouraged. Your first few briefs will be horrible, a real embarrassment, but that's to be expected. Just remember: You might brief 100 cases a week so stick with it. You will get damn good. Damn fast.

Here is your routine: read a case; re-read the case; brief it; compare it to the Case Notes. Study the difference. What did you miss? Why and how did you miss it? Figure it out. The cases you are assigned in class can take anywhere from 15 minutes to an hour to complete. In school you are on a massive time crunch. But you're not in school yet, so take your time, do it right, and master the skill now.

This practice will really give you a sense of your upcoming first semester. It's hard, but it's not just work, it's actually kind of fun. You're reading real cases. You're seeing how the real courts ruled in these real cases. You're learning the law. And since you have an interest in law, I'm willing to bet you might like doing the work. The best part, at this point, is that you don't have a deadline.

There is no pressure. And trust me that luxury is something you won't have once school starts.

9

BE PREPARED

The professor stood tall above the class as he flipped through his text book on the Podium of Power. All the students sat in fearful anticipation. Their books open, their fingers crossed, their eyes wide. All praying they wouldn't get called on.

"Let's begin," he softly stated to the deathly silent students. He calmly left the podium and began a slow, silent walk up and down the desk rows. All eyes were buried in their books. All hands were trembling beneath the desks. All ears were focused on the click of his heels – measuring his distance like bats.

I let out a meek and thankful sigh as he passed me. Happy I wasn't going to get reamed for being unprepared. Unfortunately the professor heard me. A millisecond later he turned and faced me with the look of a demented clown. With a crooked and painted smile and mocking tone he asked, "Mr. Reppas, how are you? Thank you for coming to class today."

The obvious sarcasm in his voice sent most of the students

into a very soft laughter. Of course no one dared laugh out loud for fear it would attract attention to them. No one wanted to be called on next. As the object of attack, I sat quietly and nodded my head at the professor while fumbling through my notebook as if I had something prepared.

"Why don't you present the first case for us today Mr. Reppas," the professor said, half hoping I hadn't prepared. Unfortunately for me, his dream was soon to become a reality. I kept flipping through the pages trying to buy time. It was useless, he was not going to wait.

"Well Mr. Reppas?" he kindly asked.

My delay tactics had come to an end. "Sorry professor, I can't seem to find my brief. Maybe . . . I left it at home? I am sorry." The sincerity in my voice was too perfect. He knew not to believe me. He didn't pause for a second before stating, "Then why don't you go home and look for it. Goodbye Mr. Reppas."

The class was instantly still. The professor stopped cold, staring, waiting for me to leave. There was nothing to do but collect my things as quickly as possible and leave. Talk about embarrassment. The whole class thought I was a slacker.

Damn! That's not a good way to start your day.

My friends, that is what happens to slackers. And, "NO" that never happened to me. It has happened to many, many other students in law school though, and that is something that you need to avoid. Once you get into law school the screwing around better be over. If you slack, you get tossed. And believe me, the professors will throw you out and humiliate you – every chance they get.

This is your first lesson: be prepared.

10

A Quick Summary Of My First Semester Classes

Let me tell you a bit about the classes I had my first semester of law school.

The first class was **Civil Procedure**, referred to as "Civ Pro" by all the cool kids. This class was basically about court rules for civil disputes (not for criminal cases). Rules that tell you how many days your client has to file a response with the Clerk of Court after being served with a complaint (a "lawsuit"); how many days you have to file a counterclaim (a "counter-lawsuit" against the plaintiff suing your client); what needs to be filed and when; all kinds of permissible pleadings and the corresponding filing deadlines for each. And we're talking about a ton of different motions all with different deadlines. These rules govern virtually all procedures of a lawsuit. There are Federal Rules, State Rules, Local Rules… rules, rules, rules!

This course was about how to actually practice law. This is, by far, the hardest course you will have in your first year. Every lawyer will tell you that, every upperclassman will tell you that, and every professor will tell you that. It is so tough because it is very confusing and difficult to piece together. You read and re-read all these unbelievably long cases trying to understand each one on their own. That's hard enough, but then, you have to try and piece them all together to get one "whole" picture. It's like a puzzle full of square, grey pieces that lack any identifiable couplings to help you find their connecting piece.

The guy who was ranked #1 in the third year class told me that if I didn't figure it out by Thanksgiving I was in trouble (that's three months into the four-month semester by the way). "Until then," he said, "don't worry... you're not supposed to be able to figure it out."

My second class was **Contracts**. Everybody knows what a contract is: one guy/gal promises to do something and the other guy/gal promises to do something in return. It sounds simple enough, and for some, this area of law is even fun. I think this was true, in part, because everyone had some idea of what contracts were. I also thought people liked this course because it was conceptually easier to understand than Civ. Pro.

What should have been paradise, however, was not, because our professor was an evil man – in class anyway. He was one of those professors who got in your face and intimidated the hell out of you. The kind who intentionally tried to humiliate you. The kind that threw you out of class if you failed to answer a question correctly, came in three seconds late, or just looked at him cross-eyed. This is the type of professor who believed that giving students a hard time and putting them on the spot will make them tough and teach them not to be intimidated by courtroom judges. He lived by the Socratic Method — we died by it.

This type of professor will get you to answer his way if it takes

ten minutes... and believe me those ten minutes last forever. If he calls on you, BE AFRAID... BE VERY AFRAID! He will not leave you alone until you answer the way he wants you to answer. And don't show any sign of weakness because he thrives on the weak and he will have a feast with your lack-of-confidence. If he hears even a slight tremor in your voice he will turn on you and attack. You have to answer quickly, definitively, articulately, and hopefully, correctly.

To end my quick synopsis of this class, this professor was rumored to be the hardest grader of all the first-year professors. To add to his hype, a rumor was circulated (probably by him) that he gave out nineteen "Ds" and seven "Fs" the previous year because the students "just didn't get it." Still sound like a great class?

My third class was **Torts**, which is a class that revolved around "legal wrongs" done to a person. These are basically acts done by one person that hurt another, and the victim wants monetary compensation to make them feel "whole again." For most students, this was the easiest of all first semester classes because, like Contracts, it dealt with a subject everyone already knew something about. They didn't necessarily know the correct meaning of the terms, but they all had an idea of what an "assault" was, what a "battery" was, and what the "intentional infliction of emotional distress" was.

Don't be fooled though, it is a difficult class. You will have to memorize all the "elements" of each tort, and they are countless. "Elements" is a term used to describe the core definition of a legal cause of action. As an easy example, "battery" is a "harmful or offensive touching to the person of another without his consent." A lot of memorization here.

My fourth class was **Criminal Law** ("Crim"). At the risk of ruining the surprise for you, Crim is a course about the criminal justice system. It deals with everything from rape to robbery and every other imaginable disgusting crime. This course is different from Torts, in that the defendants are not being sued for monetary compensation, rather, the State is "suing" them for breaking the law, and the punishment, if convicted, is prison.

In other words, if a guy is convicted of murder, that doesn't have anything to do with a suit by the victim's family to recover money from him. One is a criminal matter, the penalty of which is incarceration, and the other is civil, the penalty of which is a monetary judgment. Two different actions. Two different courts. Got it? Personally, I did not like this class. I am not a CSI Miami kind of guy, and for me, it was a bit too violent and graphic. Most people like it, so maybe you will too.

My last class was **Legal Writing, Analysis and Research** (commonly referred to as "LW"). This class is all about how to "write like an attorney." In this class you are given made-up facts for a case and you have to conduct your legal research. Then you have to write formal legal memoranda arguing your side. It's basically a legal writing workshop. I loved it. Go figure. In this class you write briefs, memorandums, motions, and a ton of other legal documents full of "legalese" (look it up).

11

LIFE AS A FIRST-YEAR LAW STUDENT

Once law school starts your previous life really does end. Before law school, most people have a decent social life, good friends and family, and a girl or boyfriend to spend free time with. You know, a normal, healthy, and generally happy life. If you have such a life let me congratulate you before I go on. But let me be clear, if keeping that life as-is is important to you, don't go to law school. If you decide to go, you will quickly find that you have no extra time to spend with anyone. You have time for nothing extracurricular. Really. The work load is so overwhelming that even if you do have some extra time, you won't be able to enjoy yourself because you'll be too stressed and worried about classes, classmates, outlines, assignments, grades, and professors. You just won't be able to relax. Law school is a lot of stress and it is exhausting. Spending quality time with your significant other will get tough because you simply won't have time to spend with them.

I was a single man when I arrived at law school. And to be honest, I was a bit jealous of my married classmates because

I thought if you were already married things would be easier. I thought your spouse would see you working all the time, understand how huge the commitment was, and therefore, would support you and help you reach Point "B." He or she might wish you could spend more time together, but at least they would see the big picture (short-term sacrifice for long term gain). I naively thought marriages were stronger than the pressure of law school. I was wrong.

More often than not, marriages failed and the law prevailed. You will understand why later when you read some of the stories I retell in this book. It is a sad but real ending for many law school students. Former lives completely disappear, and unfortunately, do not magically reappear at graduation. For many, law school represents the ending of one life and the beginning of a new one – for good or bad.

As far as the rigors of academic study, the worst part of my first year was the feeling that I wouldn't be able to get all my work done on time. A nearly overwhelming feeling that there was just too much work to do, too much to understand... just too much of everything! I didn't have time or make the time to go out – even on weekends. I was focused on getting to Point "B." If you are too, then understand that party time is over.

So how did I handle the stress? Well, I anticipated beforehand that there would be a serious time commitment (I think everyone anticipates that), and so I chose to attend an out-of-state law school. I reasoned that if I stayed at home, I would not be able to get away from my favorite hang-outs, or seeing my best friends, or going out with old girlfriends. I opted to move somewhere no one knew me, where I knew no one, and where I felt confident that I would not have to deal with socializing when I needed to study.

I guess you could say that was smart... if you ignore the fact that going out-of-state comes with higher tuition and living expenses. Hint: the loans for out-of-state tuition and living expenses are HUGE... ridiculously HUGE.

I moved away, very far away, from everyone and everything I knew so I could focus all my strength and energy on completing my task. When you are making these decisions, don't forget the reason you're going to law school: to become an attorney; to get to Point "B." Reaching that goal takes absolute dedication. It takes hard work and sacrifice. It requires a willingness to buckle down and forget everything else in the world. To forget that there is even a world out there.

In retrospect, I believe your ability to handle your new life is what will make or break you. I think that's what the metamorphosis is all about. I wrote a poem on this theme. Have a read:

The Measure of a Man

And what then do you do in the meantime as you sit around and wait for the climax

Nothing?

Dream?

Surely you must do something

You must spend time, pass the day

The mirror is always an option

Narcissism helps a rejected soul heal

Affectations of style build egotism

Irrespective of the facade they foster and the pain they ignore

So build the Great Wall around your heart

Drown your feelings like Atlantis

Bury them in the Sahara

Just as you will succeed in protecting yourself

You will be equally isolated

It is through defeat that a great man is measured

For any fool can win

But the Hero battles on when all seems lost

Oblivious to the hardships he must endure the obstacles he must surmount

Only he knows the value of the Prize

Only he will be content after the struggle

What is the Prize, you ask? For our purpose, it is being an attorney (Point "B"), and your sacrifice to get there will be worth it because you will walk out of school with your diploma and the knowledge you obtained after all those long coffee nights. After you get your passing Bar results, you will know that your sacrifice paid off. You will have arrived at Point "B." You will have the confidence to represent any client that walks in your office, and you will go into court knowing that you have what it takes to win. You will know the value of the Prize.

| **VOICE FROM THE FUTURE:** | You don't walk out of law school with an ability to represent any client that walks into your office. Today, when I get a new case and find that the attorney on the other side is "young," I salivate and look forward to destroying

him/her because of their lack of experience.

I mean D E S T R O Y !

There are rare exceptions to this rule. As one of my first mentors told me one fine day when I was about four years into the practice, "You don't know shit about practicing law until at least five years out!" It bothered me because I had a whole year to go before I could go see the wizard about a brain, but incredibly, as I sit here with 20 years under my belt, I have to confess that it is a fairly true statement.

Best advice: Get a job and experience first and learn how to be a lawyer. Law school teaches you how to think like a lawyer, only experience will teach you how to be a good one.

12

A Superior Professor

In class one of my study partners was captured and killed by a wrathful demon. She was well prepared – and this I can personally attest to as she and I had thoroughly read and briefed every assigned case together before class. Yet Fate chose to give her an early demise, because she was called on in the wrong class, by the wrong professor. Not just any professor, but the SUPERIOR professor (cue Jaws theme).

He called her name and made her stand in front of the class. After a full minute, he asked her to recite her brief from the first assigned case. She read her brief while trying to stop her voice from trembling. When she finished, the Superior Professor said nothing. After about thirty seconds of awkward and fearful silence, she decided to make a break for it and returned to her seat. BIG MISTAKE! The professor smiled at her coldly then asked why she sat down. There was a short pause, and we could see the blood rush to her pale face. "I was done... you didn't say anything... so I sat down..." she replied with an almost tangible fear surrounding her every word.

After another long pause, she got nervous and started to stand again. Before she was even up completely straight, he coldly responded "well.... maybe you're finished, but I'm not." That's all he said. Then he waited. He waited like a hunter armed with a machine gun who had cornered a small, defenseless rabbit in a cave. The entire class waited as well. In absolute silence. Waiting and waiting. Slowly and noticeably, the rabbit began trembling, not knowing what to do next.

No one knows exactly how long he stood there in silence, but after what seem like forever, he finally exhaled a long, contemptuous breath. He looked at her and shook his head as if to say she wasn't even worth the effort of pulling the trigger. In doing so, he made her feel worthless, and by that act, he let the entire class know that he was more than just a macho man, HE was a Superior Professor!

The seconds turned into minutes and the class remained deathly silent throughout. Everyone consumed by the drama unfolding in slow motion before them. And she stood there, the poor girl, she just stood there waiting for something to happen, but the professor did nothing. Then, he just glanced down at his papers in an obvious attempt to further confuse his prey. It was a stand-off, and she broke first. "Did you want me to re-read any part of my brief for you, Professor?" she asked humbly. Quickly and well-rehearsed came the response, "No... once was quite enough." And then came the gun fire. He rifled questions so quickly that before she finished answering one, he was already firing another. Eventually she was forced to simply answer "yes" or "no." He asked questions so obscure they would be impossible for anyone to answer. Questions which exceeded the scope of our casebooks. None of us could follow him. None of us could answer.

Hell, we didn't even understand the questions. Nevertheless, he was unstoppable.

"What is this case really about?" he asked. What kind of question is that? What is the case really about? Give me a break! The poor girl had already been standing there, fighting through her fear to tell us what she thought the case was about. What kind of question was "What is this case really about?" How insulting! I couldn't understand his cruelty. The worst part was that no matter what she answered, it wasn't good enough.

The ultimate act of barbarism came when our noble professor asked her what was clearly an unanswerable question. By this point, nearly 30 minutes into his Inquisition, she couldn't even pretend to know what he was talking about. I certainly didn't, and I'm sure no one else knew either. He kept asking question after question that flew higher and higher over our heads.

So what did she do? Well, she did what any normal, honest, and intelligent person with guts would do: she told him she didn't know. She didn't try to lie her way through by bullshitting. She answered honestly. How do you think he responded to that honesty? Did he make any effort to clarify the question or give her a hint? Maybe ask the rest of the class if they knew the answer?

Well, he did what you would expect him to do. He stared at her, shook his head, and asked if she had even read the case. No joke. He asked if she had read the case. She had spent the last 30 minutes discussing the damn case, and he had the audacity to ask if she had read it? She didn't respond. How could she? She just stood there with her mouth agape, in shock, almost as if she had watched someone kill a bunny, not accepting the fact that she was the bunny. The Superior Professor let her stand there for a few more minutes, then shook his head again, and told her to sit down. No shit. He intentionally embarrassed and demeaned her in front of the entire class without hesitation or remorse. What a guy.

This was more than a trip to Hell for the girl. It was a trip to Hell for us all. My heart was pounding and I, just like everyone else in that room, was truly scared. I was scared because I couldn't answer any of his questions either. I was scared because I thought he might call on me next.

But I was mad too. I was mad because I didn't think his tactics were necessary. I did not think it was necessary to belittle her to make his point.

In my opinion, this was not a learning environment. It was like watching a hazing at a drunken frat party. Like watching a high school bully ruin a defenseless kid. It was hard to watch. I mean, come on… we had just started our first year. We'd been thrown so much new information that there wasn't any way this Superior Professor could expect us to identify obscure principles of law that existed *between* the lines of a judge's opinion from 1870. Our classmate was sacrificed to teach us all a lesson, and to send us all a warning:

If law school is too tough, drop out… *now.*

13

A Trespass Hypothetical

Let me share a crafty Torts hypothetical. It is one of thousands you may find while actually studying torts, and it will give you an idea of the types of issues you will have to address in the class. Here it is:

An old lady owns a big plot of land in a deserted part of town. The old lady's home ("H") is located immediately in the center of the land. The property is located on an east to west street (we'll call it "Reppas Street" because I like the name). Confused? Look at Sketch Diagram #1 for a visual:

Now let's say that a big-shot group of investors wants to build a super-techno high rise on all the land north of Reppas Street. And they buy all the land around... except for the old lady's property because she refuses to sell – in spite of the large cash sums offered. It had something to do with her great-grandfather building the home and all her family having lived there for the last 150 years or some other stupid reason the investors could not understand. They needed her land though and could not complete their project without it.

You may think the developers, with no way to get what they want, decided to let the old lady live in solitude and happiness and sold all their interest in the land for one-tenth the price they paid just moved on. What a nice dream.

WRONG! This is not what happens in law school hypotheticals (or in real life). Something wild has to happen. In this hypothetical, the developers don't walk away. Instead, they decide to build around the stubborn old lady's property. In fact, they build two, 25-story buildings that surround her land and home. For extra spite, they decide to connect the two buildings by building a catwalk 20 stories up which directly crosses over the rude old lady's home. It wasn't even in the original plans! They added it in at the last minute when the crazy old bat told them that they can have her land when the "sun stops shining." That's when the idea hit them.

Those are the facts. The legal issue you must decide is whether this super-techno high rise and catwalk are "trespassing" on the selfish, old lady's land. Look at Sketch Diagram #2 before you answer:

A Trespass Hypothetical

So what do you think? Is it a trespass? Before you answer, let me pose a few guiding questions (some of which I'll answer to keep this flowing).

First question: Did anything actually touch the mean, old lady's property? ANSWER: No.

Second question: Did these evil developers physically harm her property in any way? ANSWER: No again. I know it may seem like the developers have done something wrong, but remember, in law just because it seems wrong does not mean that it is a "legal wrong." So at first blush we are led to think there is no trespass.

But, unfortunately kids, you don't know everything about how the law works. In this hypo, the developers' actions are a "legal wrong." Why? Because a person has a right to the use and enjoyment of her property. Because of the position of the building around the old lady's home, something else cannot rise. What is that thing? Don't get disgusting here, it has nothing to do with the lady's fear of being spied on by her new neighbors (in fact she likes that). Rather the answer is ... (drum roll please) ... the sun! That's right, the sun up in the sky. Since the building is located to the east and west of grandma-no-sell, she can neither see the sun rise nor set.

Think about it. Doesn't it seem logical that a property owner has a right to have the sun greet her and say good night to her? Doesn't it seem logical to assume she might get some enjoyment from watching the sun rise and fall? These are rhetorical questions because she does have that right, and that right is why the developers will have to take down their high rise and move to Texas. [14]

Let me take a sidebar here and add a comment or two for you overachievers who may have caught something unwritten in all the above. Yes, she does have a right to the air space immediately above her property. The laws of property allow an individual all the land that his property covers from the center of the earth to the far reaches of the atmosphere.[15] So because the stupid, old lady has rights to the air space immediately above her land, she can force the contractors to remove the catwalk and she could use the same argument to prevent them from building at all.

By applying what you have learned about "property rights" (*i.e.*, the "use and enjoyment" of your land), you are able to save the poor, old lady from the greedy clutches of the evil developers. And even though her kids hate her − they wanted her to sell the dilapidated, old house for 100 times what it was worth − she can stay there and watch the sun rise and set every day. Of course, she will never get to take that trip to Paris she has always dreamed

---

14 Some of you might suggest that they should have knocked her off and then bought the property from her greedy kids anyway, but that would be a hypo for a Criminal Law class, not Torts.

15 At least that was the law until the government limited your upper air distance rights to allow planes to pass through higher altitudes without violating your right- it had something to do with public interest. Look it up.

about (and her kids certainly won't pay for it now), but *c'est la vie!*

Note that the situation would have been different if the house had been built in an area where high rises already existed. In that case, she probably wouldn't have been able to make the same claim. This trespass hypothetical illustrates how just ONE application would play out. Like I said before, mine is only one of hundreds you will run through in school.

A Tort in Torts Class

Another topic in torts, "Assault and Battery," gave us trouble because the class couldn't understand what the professor was talking about in his class address, so he decided to give us a hypothetical.

He called two girls to the front of the room. He handed one a book, and told the other to knock it out of the first girl's hand. He hoped this role play would teach us that even knocking something out of a persons hand constitutes a battery. As he explained, it is an act upon another's "person."

Unfortunately, his example went astray. When the girl knocked the book out of the other one's hand, she also inadvertently knocked over an electronic recorder of a third student, who had it propped up on his desk. There was a loud crash, the record-er broke, and the entire class fell to laughter.

Things escalated as voices piped in, asking, "Was that a battery?" "Who is liable?" and "What about transferred intent?" Everyone got a good laugh; even the professor who was busy trying to put the tape recorder back together ... unsuccessfully. The professor then offered to replace the recorder if it was indeed broken. Of course he did this knowing that even if the recorder was ac-

tually broken, the student would never go and request money to replace it for fear of retribution.

Now, according to lessons we learned in that same class session, the professor was actually liable for the damage. He ordered the second student to perform the act which caused the record- er to break. That's the "respondeat superior" theory: the "master" (here, the professor), is liable for the acts of his "servant," or the student. Because the servant was following the master's orders which resulted in a tort, the professor would actually be held lia- ble for the result.

However, the professor would have a defense. He would argue that the student acted negligently in performing the act, and that that negligence was the "superseding" cause of the tort. But we can stop right there, because we know that no student would ever sue their professor for a $25 cassette player – when grades are on the line.

The moral of the story: guard your recorders with your life. And if you do use one, don't sit in the aisle seat in the front row of class. [16]

Baby-Steps in the Metamorphosis

Three weeks into law school and I can honestly say I already see my personal metamorphosis occurring. I am actually thinking like an attorney. If someone accidentally bumps into me, I im- mediately wonder if it was a battery or an assault. I'm looking at the world in a new way. I'm applying the knowledge I've already received and I want to sue everybody! I must be headed in the right direction.

---

[16] On a side note, I never really understood why people bring recorders to class. Do they really have time to listen to them? There's so much other work to do, it seems impossible to relive those glorious moments again.

A Trespass Hypothetical

The process begins quickly. You're thrown all these cases, you hear all these laws, and believe it or not, you begin to think like an attorney. The metamorphosis has begun.

One week later ...

Wasn't it Descartes who said "I brief therefore I am?" No? Well he would have had he ever gone to law school. My God, that is all I seem to ever do. At least seven or eight hours a night, every night.

The stress is kicking in.

14

The First Victim

Nothing could have prepared me for what happened in Contracts. The professor walked in two minutes before class was to begin and locked the door behind him. Those of us fortunate enough to have made it in early were immediately silent as he rapidly approached the podium. He promptly opened his notebook and called out a student's name, seemingly at random. His voice was so soft that it was almost impossible to hear.

The class remained absolutely silent. No one responded. I was not sure if the person called was in class, and I did not dare turn my head to check. No one else did either. He repeated her name. Still no response. He was just about to mark off her name when a meager voice came from the back of the room. "I'm here professor, but... I didn't get that far in the reading." How could she not have gotten that far? It was the first case assigned! The professor, always maintaining his dictatorship, threw his hands up and coldly said, "Well, you know what you have to do." There was a pause.

The rest of the class waited with sadistic anticipation. We knew she'd be thrown out, and were curious how it would play out.

Heads down, with our eyes locked on our briefs, we focused our ears and listened hard. We expected to hear her close her book, scoot back her chair, walk to the door, open it, walk out, and close it... quietly... behind her. We waited and waited, but heard nothing.

What the hell was going on? Professor Stalin was so intimidating that no one even had the guts to make eye contact with him. We stayed quiet with our eyes fixated on the pages under our noses. An unsettling amount of time passed. Finally she spoke. Her voice was now a bit more forceful as she said, "I guess you want me to leave." The professor nodded his head softly said, "Yes. Yes, I do."

"I thought you'd never ask," she replied. No shit! She actually said that. The entire class went into shock. Mouths dropped, heads raised, eyes met across the room to confirm. Could it have been that we misheard? Nope. It was true. And then as if we all realized that we were at a tennis match, the class seemed to turn back to the professor almost in unison. It was his turn to hit the ball back.

Surprisingly, the professor simply stood there and stared at the girl with a blank expression. He just waited for her to collect her books and leave. We waited too. I briefly looked around and noticed that most people had resumed their last minute effort to commit their briefs to memory in case they were called upon next.

So in this calm before the storm, the class remained focused on the sounds of the unfolding spectacle. After a few moments, we heard her shuffle some papers followed by the closing of two books (even though we only had one case book, what was the other book she had open?). Then we heard the screech of her chair (loudly), a second screech as she moved it back under her desk (loudly, again), and then the patter of her soft-soled shoes across the hard floor, until she came to the classroom door. Which, of course, was locked.

What humiliation! What if she couldn't unlock it and the professor himself had to come let her out? "Oh my God," I thought to myself, "just turn the lock and get out of here lady!"

She turned the handle, but the door did not open. She kept trying. Oh Jesus. We all waited with bated breath and prayed that she would get away before it was too late. Finally, thankfully, I heard the click. The door opened and she walked out. She may have hoped for a more graceful exit, but at least she got out.

As soon as the door closed behind her, we all exhaled and then returned our attention to our malevolent leader. He stood there shaking his head in disgust, and then lifted a pen to his chin and peered at his roll-call list. He placed a check mark on the list in an overly dramatic fashion, seemingly next to her name.

Then, he calmly placed his pen on the podium and gave us a warm smile. He told us that he was going to share a personal anecdote from his law school days. I wondered where he graduated from. The Marxist School of Law?

As he began to recount his story, the air actually became breathable. Almost refreshing. He talked to us as if we were human; friends even. Here's his story:

When our professor was in law school he had a rather cold professor, not keen on knowing students' names or checking attendance. He was, however, extremely keen on grilling students mercilessly. According to our professor's recantation, his professor would peer at the roll-call, pick a name, and beat the intellectual crap out of whoever lost the draw. (Our professor was worse. He'd beat the hell out of you, then put a nasty check mark next to your name. Anyway, back to his story.)

One day in class, the girl sitting beside our professor was called upon to be the daily sacrificial lamb. She heard her name called, but did not respond. Our professor knew the girl's name and was fully aware that she was choosing not to respond. The professor then asked if the girl was present, but no one responded. He asked again. Still no response. There was a pause, and when the old man went back to the roll to pick another name, the girl leaned over to our professor and asked, "Why is he bothering me?"

The entire class, along with our professor, burst into laughter. It was a moment of masterful comedic genius. But, the story was not over. Our professor responded to the girl by saying, "I have no idea." Again, he laughed. The class followed his cue and bellowed in joyous support. What a bunch of ass-kissers.

The worst part was that I laughed too. In retrospect, I can't tell you why. The story was stupid. Nervous laughter, perhaps? I think that his speaking to us as semi-humans was enough to win us over. I wonder if that's how Stalin did it in Russia.

When the laughter died down, the professor resumed his serious tone. He told us that if any one of us ever attempted to pull off the same stunt we would be in "bad shape." He promised he would make us "pay." The room went deathly silent and we turned our attention back to the casebooks and our worthless briefs.

By the way, he threw out two more students from class that day... and put nasty, check marks by their names.

The First Victim

A Slacker Indeed

Not to belabor the point, but here's a vignette that serves as a perfect example of how a lack of motivation can affect your grades.

Most every student has at least one class that (s)he really doesn't like. At least that is true for the One-Ls because we don't get to choose our classes. Whatever that class is that you like the least (dare I say hate), it is invariably the toughest. You don't understand it, don't care about it, and don't want to spend time on it.

This class, for me, was Legal Writing, Analysis, and Research.[17] This is ironic because, as a writer, I expected to enjoy a writing class. Forget it. This class is all about learning to write "as an attorney." Grammar and style are worthless.

The professor was a joke; he was the most anally retentive person on Earth. He tried to be nice, but nobody could stomach his Mr. Rogers goodwill. We're in law school for goodness sake! Why would you present a hypothetical to adults with case names like "Flintsone v. Rubble?" and "Hatfield v. McCoy?" Incredibly unoriginal, but the worst part is that the professor actually thinks they're funny. Joke's on him.

One day we had to take a Bluebook examination. The ubiquitous Bluebook is basically a guide (that happens to be blue) for composing proper citations. It's a "How To…" guide for footnotes, end notes, and other legal references. It is boring as Hell.

Because this isn't a doctrinal class, you wouldn't expect it to take as much or more time as say Contracts or Torts. But that is exactly what happens.

I finished the test about five minutes faster than Tiffany, one of

---

17 It might be called something different at your school, but just about all law schools require some sort of Legal Writing course for first year students.

my study partners. Here I must confess that I DID NOT STUDY AT ALL FOR THAT EXAM. Why? Because I COULDN'T DO IT. I just couldn't open up that effing book and study that boring stuff. Tiff (with two "fs" she once told me), and almost everyone else,- studied like dogs for that test. I hated it so much that I couldn't bear to crack open the book's binding. Stupid? Damn right. The most I ever managed to study for that class was right before class.

When you have an anally retentive teacher like ours, you realize that he wants every period, comma, space, and underline included in your answer. Therefore, I was forced to accept that invariably I would get a few wrong. So I figured that if he was going to take off points for such minuscule errors, then so be it. Let him go crazy. Let him nitpick his way to Heaven. Why should I lose sleep over it? So I spent my entire weekend briefing cases for my other classes.

Tiff, on the other hand, did the exact opposite. She studied the Bluebook all weekend. She didn't sleep much, didn't do any other assignments, didn't see the light of day. I, meanwhile, was fresh and ready to BS my way through the exam.

Final note, I got a B+, Tiff got a B –. Go figure.

VOICE FROM THE FUTURE: Kids, you don't want to risk what I did by not studying for an exam, however insignificant or annoying the class may seem to you at the time. I got lucky, but don't let that convince you that slacking works. It's a gamble. I recommend taking the safe bet: put all your effort into every class and be judged knowing you gave it your best.

The First Victim

A Pop Quiz?

What? A pop quiz? In law school? Yes. A pop quiz in law school. And to make it worse, it was in Civ Pro!

Our homework assignment was to prepare (brief) a number of cases. The assignment was a typical one and I briefed them all. How well I understood them, however, was a different story.

The quiz was cumulative of all we had covered from the beginning of the semester. The professor said it wouldn't factor into our final grade, and was meant only to gauge how much we actually had learned in class so far. No big deal... until I looked at it. No... it was a very big deal. There was no way this guy went through the trouble of writing a five-page, multiple choice exam for it to have no effect on our grades. No way. This was real.

I have no idea how well I did. Every answer choice seemed to be a possible correct answer. I may have gotten them all right or completely bombed it. What makes this unfair was that the professor hit us with the quiz on the same day we had our daunting Bluebook exam in Legal Writing class. No doubt he knew we had that exam, and no doubt he chose this day intentionally. What a guy.

He probably guessed (correctly, I would add) that the majority of us pulled all-nighters preparing for the Bluebook exam, and consequently, had not prepared for his class. I'm sure he wanted to ream anyone who didn't prepare. The problem with a Civ Pro exam, though, is that even if you do diligently read and brief the material, there is still a pretty good chance you'll bomb. Especially when every answer seems plausible.

Monastic Life and the Complete Devotion to Law

Whether to slack off or study so much you never sleep are the two extremes of law school, but I'll tell you something: you have to keep a balance. You have to have a life outside of school to keep your mind. You have to have some fun. You have to get away from time to time and free your mind from all the law you are being fed.

A lot of law students, like me, play sports a couple times a week with other students. Some jog. Some walk. Others just watch TV.

But woe to the man who never leaves campus. Woe to he who stays on the grounds day after day, eating the same garbage cafeteria food, breathing the same unpleasant air. Sometimes you need to go out and blow off a little steam. Have a couple of beers. Hit the dance floor and shake your booty.

Don't delude yourself into believing, as I did, that you will be able to devote yourself completely to studying or that you don't need to go out and relax, because you do.

VOICE FROM THE FUTURE: Unless you are a monk don't live in a monastery. Take some time to relax and stay fresh. Find balance in the Force my Padawan.

15

Civ Pro Hell

I had a little problem in Civ Pro: I didn't know what the hell was going on. Okay, it was more than a little problem. Apparently I was not the only student who was so lost, but I was the only one I was worried about.

It's funny, because I read and briefed all the cases and really thought I understood them. Until I realized I didn't. I walked into every class deluding myself into thinking I was prepared. I knew the facts, the issues, and had the rules of law for each case, but I couldn't figure out how they were all related to each other. Invariably, when I walked out of class I realized I had no freaking idea what was white and what was black. I asked myself how it was possible that before class I had just a few questions on my briefs, but I walked out with a hundred more?

It's crazy to think that going to class actually leaves you more confused than had you not gone at all.

Of course, there were always those intellectual giants in class who seemed to know and understand everything – I hated them.

But, in truth, if we didn't have them to volunteer answers to the professor, we (the slow-witted majority) would undoubtedly be forced to actually participate in class. And that would be a far worse price to pay than simply being lost. I'd rather be lost than embarrassed in front of my peers. Peers who, no doubt, I would run across in a courtroom someday, and who would inevitably remember me getting ripped to shreds for being incompetent in school. The reality I came to accept was that I could not see the "big picture" in the class… and this was a big problem! I had to fix this problem before it got any worse.

I decided to go talk with the professor about a better preparation strategy. Here's what he told me: "When you're briefing cases in Civil Procedure, you need to brief the cases in a short form. Basically you need to get an idea of what is going on. Write down the facts. Write down the issues and the holdings. Understand those first" (this much I had done). "Then you hit the Federal Rules of Civil Procedure (which is a giant, thousand-odd page book full of very dry procedures), and then hit the Supplement (to our text book) hard. Understand what the rules are, how they apply, and how they are contradictory. Finally you need to really think about why the case was decided the way it was. What were the Supreme Court Judges trying to do and why? Do their dissenting opinions support other theories or new trends that the law is taking? You need to learn what the judges are thinking."

That's it? That's all I need to do? No problem. I was sure I'd ace this class (heavy, heavy sarcasm here).

Yes, I know the prof seemed like a nice guy. Very helpful. And at least my section didn't have to memorize all 86 Rules of Civil Procedure. As another professor required just that from his students. No shit. The other section had to memorize all that boring drivel, and be able to produce it all on their final exam. I guess we didn't have it that bad after all, and our exam was even open book. Like that would help! An open book exam is useless unless you actually know what the hell is in the book.

I also asked him about using a Hornbook or other supplemental material to help with understanding.[18] Remember, this very professor and others explicitly told us never to use these materials. In my case, he didn't tell me to use a Hornbook, but he also didn't tell me not to. In fact, he didn't say anything at all. He just repeated that I need to understand the "big Civ Pro picture." Since he apparently wouldn't be teaching that in his boring class, I had no alternative but to buy a Hornbook and teach it to myself.

At least I now had a strategy which, I hoped, would finally help me understand what Civ Pro was really all about.

| VOICE FROM THE FUTURE: | 100% necessary: buy a Hornbook for this class. I would buy it the day you get your acceptance letter to law school. The Hornbook I bought was called, not surprisingly, "Civil Procedure," published by West Publishing. I still have it to this day. I don't use it much now, but I keep it in case I have a case with complicated jurisdiction issues that I need to outline. A wise investment to understand a very difficult class for the newbie and a permanent addition to the bookshelf in your future law office.

---

18 A "Hornbook," in case you don't know, is a huge text book written by legal scholars which "summarizes and simplifies" specific areas of law. There's one for every class, field, and topic.

16

Two More Fun Hypotheticals

As I trust you gathered from the earlier vignettes you have read so far, a very common tool professors use to help students apply case law to real life is called a hypo ("hypothetical").

A hypo is a scenario – usually very simple – made up by the professor and intended to help a student better understand the topic being discussed by having them apply the legal concept to a made-up story. You'll have hypos in every class, for every new rule. I'll give you two quick ones to consider.

The first is a Contract hypo where a minor (under 18 years old) purchased an automobile and later tried to *avoid* [19] the contract. Now the cases you have read and briefed so far in this first semester have clearly led you to believe that the law is clear on this subject: a minor cannot be bound by any contract because he is not mature enough in the eyes of the law to be legally bound to its terms, as would an adult. So my professor gave us the same facts, but added that the person seeking to avoid the contract is

---

19 A "legal" way of saying "get out of."

no longer a minor. He bought the car when he was seventeen, but is now is eighteen and trying to cancel the contract by saying he was a minor at time of purchase, and therefore that the contract was "voidable" (important legal word there). The reason he wants to return the car and avoid the contract is immaterial. The hypo is a practice in answering the following question: can someone who is now the age of majority, avoid a contract on the basis that he or she was a minor (and therefore "incompetent" to enter into a contract) at the time of contract formation? Think about it and then read the footnote at the bottom of the page here to find your answer. [20]

The second hypo takes you on a journey to consider a Tort concept called "strict liability." Strick liability is applied by the courts in cases where a seller of goods is liable for any and all defective or hazardous products which unduly threaten a consumer's personal safety. Here's a hypo: If a tree removal company uses dynamite to blow out a stump from a house across the street, and the shock from the explosion shatters the glass of your 1971 Pinto, is the company liable to you for those damages? Applying Tort laws to the hypo, you should conclude that the tree removal company would be strictly liable, even though nothing physically involved in the blast caused the damage.

Good stuff. Keep moving on.

---

20 Yes. He can get out of the contract.

17

The First Major Assignment

Law School – Week Six. Closed Memo due.

This Legal Research and Writing assignment covered six different issues relating to landlord and tenant agreements, housing code violations, and basic conditions of a leased premises. It was worth 25% of our overall class grade. We were given one week to complete it. This, coupled with the fact that we were (dare I say "intentionally") given extensive assignments due in all other classes made our stress levels skyrocket.

Personally, I was unable to even begin the assignment until three days before the deadline. I managed to complete the assignment on time by pulling one all-nighter and two nights of three-hour sleep. In fact, I managed to turn in the memo three full minutes before the deadline. I had to sprint across campus to make it, but I made it, and that's what counts.

Regarding the deadline, we were expressly told by the Writing department to turn in the assignment between 11 a.m. and 12 noon that Monday. We were told that anything turned in after 12:01 p.m. would be dropped in grade considerably, based on how late it was turned in.

Many people were not as fortunate as I in meeting the deadline. In fact one of my study partners had quite an ordeal. She did manage to finish it, but turned it in 8 minutes late. She had a very good reason for this: her computer had blown up and she had no way to type the memo. I let her use my computer, and she worked non-stop from 7 a.m. until she finished.

At first, the secretary to whom we were supposed to hand in the memo, refused to accept it. Knowing she was being toyed with, she protested. The woman didn't budge, and my study partner persisted. "This is ridiculous, I was just a few minutes late, you have to take it." The secretary finally acquiesced, and informed my partner that for every ten minutes the memo is late, the grade is dropped by a letter. Because she fell within the first ten-minute spot, my partner was only going to lose one letter grade. That means the best she could hope for was a "B."

If you consider that 25% of your grade was fully dependent on this one paper, having an entire letter grade dropped is tremendous. Especially considering how much time was spent preparing the damn thing.

Let's put it this way. The effect this had on my study partner epitomizes the negative attitude I have toward "superior professors" who make it their life goal to give One-Ls the hardest time possible. My poor partner was a nervous wreck. She was scared. She had to run all the way across campus crying because she knew she was late, and then got reamed and dropped a letter grade by the secretary! Did she deserve that? Was it really necessary to put her through that? Did it make them feel good that she broke down and cried?

I had been waiting for my study partner outside the office. Even from there, you could hear students fighting with that poor secretary who had to do the professors' dirty work. And sadly, my partner wasn't the only one late. There were other students who were obviously in the same boat.

There were quite a few people crying, in fact, and I felt like crying too. It's not a pretty sight when stress breaks a person. Some students thought the deductions were fair; these were, naturally, the students who managed to turn them in on time. Their reasoning was that everybody knew when the memo was due, and almost everybody turned it in on time. Their thinking was something like: "why shouldn't those who didn't meet the time requirement be penalized?" and, "I turned it in on time, so why should those who didn't get rewarded for not complying with the rules? Those slackers. Shouldn't they pay?"

No they shouldn't. At least not that way. Not in my opinion. There is a fine line between penalizing and butchering. I guess the excuse that the "superior professors" will undoubtedly fall back on is that if you are late to court, you lose the case. They reason that law school should be no different. Maybe. But just a few minutes late most probably will not result in a loss in court. Judges will hear and consider the reason for the tardiness. And being a few minutes late might not matter after all. Then again maybe it will. I don't know. All I know is that I think the way that the system works is cold, uncaring, and meant to break a student, not build them up.

So what can you learn from this? Why do professors act this way toward first year law students? Believe it or not, there is more to it than just court preparation. Their punishments – drilling us, throwing us out of class, docking points – are administered intentionally. They want to put us through the wringer.

Some of the "superior professors" brag about their actions to second and third year students. No joke. My upper class friends tell me that our professors share their punishment anecdotes, and laugh when they describe how scared we were. Isn't that lovely? Sound like something you can handle? It better be. Stress management is not a joke. Law school is not a vacation. When you get to Law School you better be prepared to do your work and handle the pressure or don't go.

By the way, by week seven, two people dropped out from my section. No one knows precisely why, but we all assumed it had to do with the stress. Both of my study partners questioned whether they could handle it anymore. I wonder how many other students wondered the same thing.

It was a tough weekend. Very tough. Thankfully the first big assignment was over and now we could all move forward. I was still there, and most everybody else was, too. We were all a bit tougher and a bit smarter.

Everyone said that if you could make it through the first semester of law school, you could make it through the whole three years.

I finally understood what they meant.

18

A Brief Musical Interlude

Law School: The Musical[21],
Scene 2: "One-L Life"

Main character is awakened by the all too familiar beeping and buzzing sounds of his demonic alarm clock. He strikes the machine with a precise blow of his hand, causing it to wince in pain and immediately stop its shrieking. Main character then rolls back over in an attempt to reestablish the link he had with the desert island,

---

21 **VOICE FROM THE FUTURE:** Yes. I wrote a musical. I wrote it as my legal writing assignment in a class I took as a Three-L called "Law & Literature." The assignment was completely open and the students were allowed to write a paper or take a final written exam. I chose the paper because the professor let us write whatever kind of paper we wanted: a biography of a famous judge; a legal paper; or, in my case, a musical. We were allowed to write whatever we wanted as long as it had a tie to both "law" and "literature." I am including a few scenes from my "paper" in this book, to break up the monotony a bit and because all of the experiences I wrote about directly or indirectly relate to Law School and/or to the legal jargon used by students and practitioners of the "Law." What probably helped me get the "A" that I did (hold your applause, please), was because I added "end notes" wherein I listed all the sources I used, and when appropriate, explained any cases I referred to, legal concepts I discussed, and legal terminology that a non-lawyer would not completely understand. I included the endnotes at the end of every scene and I include them in this book, also for your review.

the sandy beach, and the parade of bikini waitresses. Unfortunately, however, the noncomplying clock begins another frantic episode of its shrilling beeps and buzzes. Main character again strikes the machine with a fury, but this time he does not attempt to go back to sleep. Instead he decides to leave his blissful dream-world in favor of the cold reality known as One-L life. He realizes that there is no escape.

After showering and dressing, the main character opens the blinds in his apartment, (although it is debatable whether a tiny room in the dorms with an old, creaky bed, battered desk and unclean bathroom actually qualifies as an "apartment"). The sun is just breaking on the horizon and the main character heaves a heavy sigh and murmurs out: "well, here we go again." It is now 6:15 in the morning as he begins his walk to the law library.

There are four study groups already at the library when he arrives. The groups are hotly debating their subject matter as they prepare for their first-year classes. The main character's group is among them, and he joins them as they are engaged in discussion over the Contracts cases they are to have prepared for their 7:30 a.m. class.

Study
Partner #1:   I'm not really sure that I've got this all straight
           A child can avoid a contract until their ten plus eight

(Dueling Sonnets)

Study
Partner #2:   That's the law, that's the rule
           And that's all we're supposed to learn in school
           Since minors aren't as smart and capable
           Contracts they enter into are voidable

A Brief Musical Interlude

Although offer, acceptance, and consideration

Should also be discussed in our deliberation
The bottom line is not a question of fact
It's a rule: anyone under eighteen can avoid a contract

Haven't you yet understood the Golden Rule of School
You see, the trick to passing the Bar Exam
Is to learn all the majority rules of law
And ignore all the concurrences and dissents

That's where I'll focus all of my time
That's all I need, with that I'll be fine

Study
Partner #1:   You know . . . I couldn't disagree more

Going to Law School is more than passing a Bar Exam
It's more than just learning the rules
You're taking a "status quo" approach to life
In your fallacious interpretation of the Golden Rule

The "law" is something that is never forever the same
And as our society grows and becomes more diverse
What was moral when the law was written yesterday
If upheld today would be an evil curse

Not so many years ago there was no universal suffrage
We lived in a society where separate was equal
And if we had stuck with that rule
Then most Americans would still be oppressed people

Studying all dissents shows how the law may change
Your Golden Rule of Law School must reflect that aim

103

The two study partners continue their debate but their voices leave our ears. Main character then rises and begins the chorus in a soliloquy.

Chorus: *Oh yes, it's six fifteen*
             And I'm tired and weak
             But I have to think and think

             Though I am not quite sure
             That debate is the cure
             I am forced to endure and endure

             This is One-L Life
             My ball and chain new wife
             My life as a first-year slave

             One-L Life
             Full of suffering and strife
             Always studying though sleep depraved

Main character rejoins his study group, as another student from a nearby study group stands and begins his soliloquy.

Student #1:   What the Hell is Civ Pro
              I don't have a clue
              Something about "minimum contacts"
              Denckla, Woodson, and Shoe
              Ask my friends around me
              They claim to have the solution
              But every word of explanation
              Just adds to my confusion

A Brief Musical Interlude

Chorus :   *Yes, it's six fifteen*
(all students)   *And we're tired and weak*
                  But we have to think and think

                  Though we are not yet sure
                  That debate is the cure
                  We are forced to endure and endure

                  This is One-L Life
                  Our ball and chain new wives
                  Our lives as first-year slaves

                  One-L Life
                  Full of suffering and strife
                  Always studying though sleep depraved

The student then retakes his seat with his study partners. Two new students from the last two study groups rise and begin singing a duet.

Student #2 (speaking): Criminal Law . . . ohhh

Student #3 (speaking): Property . . . uhhh

(Students #2 and #3
singing
simultaneously): My first-year professor holds me in captivity

Student #2: I feel I'm being punished, though I'm without culpability (crim. law)

Student #3: With present and future interests, and alienability (property)

Student #2: I lack the intent, but to prevent any possibility (crim. law)

Student #3: I study fee-simple, life estates, and inheritability (property)

(simultaneously): My professor is bent on bending my sense of ability

Chorus Repeat & Outro

The scene ends as all the students return to their study groups and continue to prepare for their classes.

<u>END NOTES</u>:

"Minors" refer to anyone who is under the age of "majority," *i.e.,* anyone who is under eighteen – although the age may vary from state to state. The "Law" refers to these people as "children" and allows them to get out of contracts they enter into with adults. For example, if a ten-year-old signs a contract with a moped salesman to buy the motorized bike, that same minor can escape his obligation to pay off the bike if he loses or quits his paper route (or any other reason). The courts allow these children to "avoid" these contracts because of their youth and immaturity. Thus, when an adult enters into a contract with a minor, he must realize that the contract is not binding upon the youth, as it would be with an adult. All the child need do is return the bike and tell the adult that he no longer wants the responsibility of the contract he entered into. For a further analysis, refer to the case of Pettit v. Liston, 97 Or. 464, 191 P. 660, (Or. 1920).

"Civ Pro," "Minimum Contacts," and "Denckla, Woodson, and Shoe" all refer to concepts and cases studied in the first-year course Civil Procedure. The course itself is all about jurisdiction and the rules you have to follow to file a lawsuit and everything else you can imagine about representing a client and going to court. "Minimum Contacts" is a concept which, basically, says that in order for the court to be able to make an out of state (or out of country) person or company appear in their court, they have to have a certain number of ties with the state in which they are being compelled to appear in. The three main cases that deal with this concept are: Hanson v. Denckla, 357 U.S. 235, 78 S.Ct. 1228, 2 L.Ed. 1283 (1958); World-Wide Volkswagen Corp. v. Woodson, 444 U.S. 286, 100 S.Ct. 559, 62 L.Ed.2d 490 (1980); and Int'l Shoe Co. v. Washington, 326 U.S. 310, 66 S.Ct. 154, 90 L.Ed. 95 (1945).

"Present and future interests," "alienability," "fee-simple," "life estates," and "inheritability" are all concepts relating to property law. For a more detailed description of these concepts refer to: Lawrence and Minzner, Student's Guide to Estates in Land and Future Interests, 1991.

19

The Frustrated Professor

I went to see the Property professor. I wouldn't take Property until the following semester, so I didn't know her personally, but I heard she had a doctorate in English. This, of course, got me curious, and I wanted to ask her about what I needed to do to become a published writer.

I'd been writing for years, but never tried to get any of my writings published. I thought that as an intelligent and encouraging teacher she could give me some tips. I thought that as a member of the literary world she might be willing to introduce me to someone; be a mentor. Mentor; help; you understand.

With that goal in mind I knocked on her office door and introduced myself. I told her why I came to see her and what I hoped she could do for me. Being a young man, far from home and with no connections, I was sure she'd be willing to help. I was excited, happy and extremely polite. She was not.

I handed her a collection of some of my best poetry. Yes I did. I know… that's about as nerdy as you can get. Anyway, my point is that it takes nerve to hand someone your work for review and critique. And it wasn't a plain, elementary school 3-hole punch, dollar store, notebook that I handed her either. It was bound, with a professionally painted and designed cover [22] . . . and looked damn impressive.

She barely glimpsed at it before handing it right back.

Ouch! I had hoped she would take it home and read a couple of poems, or at least skim through the text right there. She did neither. She simply handed it back with absolutely no expression on her face. I didn't know what to do so I just stood there, waiting. She told me that there was no point to continue writing creatively. She said that by the time I finished law school, I would never be able to write creatively again.

"Law school changes your perspectives so much that you are unable to write anything unrelated to law," she said with a joyless sincerity. Even though she was expressionless and her voice was dull and monotone, she was sincere. She meant what she said.

I asked if she had been a creative writer in the past. She said yes. I asked if she stopped after graduating law school. She said she stopped while in law school. I kind of shook my head and asked her a somewhat redundant question: "And you've written nothing since?" She answered with one word: "correct." I then asked her if it bothered her to no longer be writing creatively. She told me it took her a number of years to accept. . . and left it at that. She didn't finish her sentence, and I really didn't want to hear any more. I thanked her for her time, apologized for the intrusion, and left.

It took me some time to sort through that experience. I felt it

---

22 Credit for the cover to "The Politics of Contemplation" goes to my old friend, Rob Schaeffer.

was another cruel and unnecessary law school lesson. I was upset and hurt by how she treated me. Not because I felt she was lying to me, indeed, I felt she was telling me what she believed to be the truth, but rather, because she was taking her failure and applying it to me as if it were a legal precedent. I failed and, therefore, so will you. That's the law.

She was saying that since she couldn't be a creative writer after attending law school, I couldn't either. She didn't know me from Adam. She didn't know what type of writer I was or if I was even any good. She knew nothing about me. She seemed to say that if I wanted to be a writer, then I shouldn't be in law school.

Moments like that made me wonder that if I brought my sick, old dog to school whether there would be a line of professors there to kick her.

20

My Interrogation

Guess who got called on in Civ Pro? That's right. Me! It was now the eighth week of the first semester and I finally got reamed. Well, not reamed. Let's just say that I got called on – unannounced – to present a case and argue against the professor. I was put on the "hot seat." How did it go? Read on.

The old professor walked into class, and took his now familiar stance behind the podium. He looked at his book briefly, and then posed a question apparently to the entire class with his usual, boring, monotonous tone. After he posed his question, he turned to and pointed directly at me.

"Mr. Reppas, what's the answer?" [Insert ominous music here]

Was I bothered? Was I scared or nervous? Well… yes, of course, but in spite of that initial shock I looked at my brief and thought, for some reason, that I knew the answer. I responded in a slow, deep voice, and did my best to show no sign of fear or uncertainty.

Turns out my answer was right. Or, at least, my answer was acceptable. I actually thought, since I had given an "acceptable" answer, that I was off the hook. Not at all. He didn't miss a beat to ask a follow-up. I looked down again, and again felt blessed by angels because again, I thought I knew the answer. He nodded his head before firing the next question.

This one, unfortunately, was way out of my league. I had no idea how to answer. I think professors intentionally ask "unanswerable" questions whenever students are on a roll. I guess it brings the student back to earth and reminds the class who is King and who are the peasants. But I didn't give in. I paused and put on a decent performance pondering the answer. I had to give him an answer as I'm not the type to to say, "I don't know." [23]

I watched him and he watched me. A stare down between hunter and prey. A mental battle between this legal god and his young apprentice.

I had brought a nice, big cup of coffee with me to class (my standard routine) and, don't ask me why, but the next thing I knew, I was casually taking a sip from it. Oh yes, I was that fearless. Then I gave him my answer. Which wasn't really an answer, it was

---

[23] VOICE FROM THE FUTURE: It happens to everyone from time to time. There have been a few instances in my career where a judge asked me a legal question that I didn't know the answer to. It happens. You have to deal with it. Sometimes you don't know the answer because the law is not clear, other times its simply because you don't know. In either case, here is a great tip on how to answer questions like that, respond as follows: "That is an interesting question your Honor, and one that I did not address in my motion. I don't think the answer is a simple one, so I would ask the Court to allow me to submit a Memorandum of Law on this point and reserve on ruling until you can review and consider same." Now don't be fooled, if your judge asks you a question that is part of the arguments you or your opposing counsel are arguing at the hearing, the judge will likely make you look like a fool for not knowing the answer (and you'll probably lose your client if they attend the hearing with you), but if it's a new issue being discussed, judges are generally willing to let the parties research the law for them. Ultimately, they want to be right in their ruling, so they look at these situations as learning experiences for everyone – themselves included. Most of them are not the Superior Professor types; there is professionalism out there.

more of a counter-question: "Well, that depends on how you look at it." Now, most professors do not allow students to ask questions. They insist you figure it out for yourself. In this case, however, I think that because the professor knew I couldn't possibly answer his question with my limited knowledge of civil procedure, he let me slide.

So, I proceeded to argue virtually every side of the issue I thought he wanted to hear. And guess what? Somehow, I actually ended up answering the question he originally asked and managed to include rules of law from other cases, and showed how they each applied in the case at bar.[24]

Damn did I hit the ball, or what? But instead of a "congratulations" or "good job," he went directly to a new question. And that's how my inquisition progressed. He'd give me about 30 seconds to answer before interrupting with a follow-up. 30 seconds. Question. 30 seconds. Question. 30 seconds. And so on.

I did my best to stay calm through my interrogation. It wasn't easy, and I had to continuously focus on my speaking voice: "Keep it deep, keep it loud, stay articulate." And finally, epiphany! Can you believe it – he finally called on someone else! Thank God. Or should I say, "Thank you professor?"

After class, my study partners told me what a hell of a job I had done. A few other peers gave me the same praise. Although I didn't know it at the time, apparently the entire class was lost during the saga. They were flipping through their notes and texts like a sinner on judgment day trying to find something in the Bible that might save him.

Don't ask me how, but somehow I had everything the pro-

---

24 "Case at bar" is a fancy legalese term meaning "the present case."

fessor wanted, all neatly typed out on my three-page brief. Did I finally understand this elusive class, or was it just luck?

Yes, the light bulb turned on that day. I knew it then and there, and so did everyone else.

21

Attorney Encounters
of the Third Kind

I was in the library working on a legal writing assignment[25] when something odd happened. But first, the assignment (nothing new): I was given a fact pattern and told to research any legal issues I spotted and find cases that supported or refuted those issues. So there I was in the library, muddling my way through rows and rows and rows and rows of legal books. I went from Supreme Court decisions, to state court decisions, to treatises, to dictionaries, to reporters, to books about the Congress and Senate, to American Journals – everything you could imagine. It was confusing and I was lost. I was also a bit upset, because the stupid assignment was taking way too much time to finish. Legal Research and Writing classes always take precious time away from the other substantive (*i.e.*, "important") classes. So now back to: the Encounter (cue in *The Twilight Zone* theme).

I went to the reference desk to ask for help finding a book. The librarian was speaking to a guy, about 35 years old, really

---

25 Which, like all others, sucked.

overweight, well-dressed. When finally acknowledged, I asked the librarian about the book I was looking for. After explaining my problem to the librarian, this unknown, well-dressed dude interrupted us to say that he would be happy to show me where to find the book.

I told him it wasn't necessary, but he insisted and started off. I followed him through the labyrinth as he led me directly to the book. I thanked him and he said, "No problem. I went through this myself not too long ago, so I remember how tough it was. Let me walk you around this place and explain it to you real quick."

"Great, you really don't have to, but thanks a lot." So the tour began.

We walked around and he pointed out books and told me what they were and what I needed them for. Of course I retained about 0% of what he was telling me, but I pretended to be enthused.

It turns out, my guide graduated the year before I started, and was now a sole practitioner. He asked where I was from, what my plans for the future were, and how I was enjoying the Law School experience. Blah, blah blah.

Then he asked, "How is Torts going?"

"Great, just great."

"Yeah?" he said dubiously. Then out of nowhere, he asked me a Torts question. "Do you know what the elements are of Battery?"

"Elements," for those who don't know, are specific things that have to be present for an offense to have legally occurred (in this case a battery). The elements of battery are: (1) an intention to cause a harmful or offensive contact to another person; (2) the apparent ability to cause such contact; and (3) the contact actually occurs. So, in order to prove a battery has occurred, you must show that the perpetrator (or "tortfeasor" in legalese) intended to cause the contact, that the victim thought the tortfeasor could actually cause such harm, and that some harmful contact, in fact, occurred. Got it? Good. Now back to the story.

I was stunned. Was he quizzing me?! In any case, I answered the question, and then he asked me another. "What about Negligence?"

I told him, "First, you have to show that there was a duty owed by the actor to the victim. Second, you have to show that the actor breached that duty. Thirdly, you have to show that the breach of that duty was the cause of the victim's injury. And lastly, you have to show that the injury sustained resulted in damages."

He nodded, smiled, and then got to the point. It should have been obvious that he was not wasting his time on me out of the goodness of his heart. He was, after all, an attorney. I should have realized sooner he had another motive.

He told me that he was interested in having some students work for him. "You know, do some research, make some extra money. It's a good experience. Plus, I won't have to come in at night and do it myself. What do you say?"

I told him I wasn't hurting for money, so I wasn't really gung-ho about working, especially during my first semester. Then he asked who I had for Civ Pro, and I told him. Turns out, he had had the same professor, and was now offering me his old outline. Yes kids, he said the magic word: Outline! Ooh, bells are ringing and the plot is thickening. He also had one for Contracts. Man can this guy set the right bait or what?! We exchanged phone numbers and I told him I would give him a call.

So now what? Where did that leave me? Should I go for the outlines from someone who, obviously, passed these classes? Outlines that would save me hours and hours of work[26].

So I thought to myself, "Self, what kind of research would a practicing attorney want a first-year law student to do anyway? What does this guy really want from me? Hell, he knows I don't even know my way around the library! Then it dawned on me, "He wants my Lexis and West Law numbers!" Absolutely. What else could it be?

What is Lexis and West Law, you ask? Well, they are the two major online legal databases of every case that has ever been decided and published by every U.S. court. They also contain every state and federal law, every statute, and every other imaginable secondary source of legal information. All that info on your very own computer screen and out from your very own printer. So why doesn't this guy just get his own account? Well because while access to these databases is free for students, attorneys have to pay about $6 a minute. No shit. That's big money, especially for a sole practitioner. That also explains why they give the service for free to students: so that we use it all the time and get hooked. When students can do all their research online, they never put in the effort to learn how to browse through actual books containing all the same information. The students get trained to do it without any heavy lifting, and by the time they graduate they have no choice but to pay for the service. At $6 a minute, it's a great marketing strategy.[27]

---

26 I'm guessing of course, as I have yet to create an outline. My understanding is they take hours, if not days, to complete.

27 VOICE FROM THE FUTURE: In my present day practice, I have what's called the "Florida Litigator's Package," which gives me all the case law, statutes, rules, etc., that I need to practice as a litigator in Florida. It costs my firm about $400/month, flat rate, no matter how much I use it.

Attorney Encounters of the Third Kind

My guess was this guy wanted to scam my passwords in exchange for outlines, and presumably some cash. Sound like a good deal? WRONG. It would be a breach of contract for me to use, or allow someone else to use, the service for any non-school related work. The companies could potentially cancel my account, and charge me for every minute already spent online. The school and the Bar, on the other hand, would be much, much less forgiving. I could easily get expelled. In the best case scenario, in which I did manage to graduate, the Bar would probably never admit me. If I let the guy use my account, or even if I used it on his behalf, the Bar would consider it theft, and no state Bar admits a thief. He probably worked for Lexis anyway.

So what did I do? Don't forget I was new to this state, and needed every connection I could make. I also would have loved to get a couple of outlines for these tough classes.

I decided to talk to the Assistant Dean of the law school, who also happened to be my Civ Pro professor. I didn't use names, but I did tell him the situation as well as my concerns. He told me that, actually, there wasn't really a problem. I could work for the guy (although not my first semester, because no one was allowed to work their first semester), I just couldn't give him my passwords. He recommended I don't work at all, but said the choice was mine.

He also told me to proceed with caution. "If at any point you feel as if you are at a moral crossroads, it is not worth it to risk your future for an outline and some cash." He then went into a five minute speech on the harm that using someone else's outlines would have on my grades. I nodded a lot until I found the right moment to thank him and excuse myself.

Ultimately, I decided to pass and keep all my attention on the Law School Game I was playing.

22

Brief Trouble and Outlines

Indicators That You're About To
Have Trouble Briefing a Case

You know a case is going to be difficult to read and brief when you have to look up the FIRST FOUR WORDS! If you spend five minutes going through Black's[28] to figure out the opening sentence, that's a hint for how the rest will go. Warning lights begin to flash. This is going to suck.

Outlines

Outlines are study guides for every exam you are going to take in law school. It is a term you will hear constantly. Outlines organize lecture notes, text notes, and briefs into a single concise summary. It's basically the best tool for exam prep, and everyone will be talking about outlines from Day One.

---

28 That is, of course, Black's Law Dictionary.

Personally, I never really understood how outlines were different from high school, undergrad, or even grad school study guides. To a large extent, law school outlines are not very different. The major difference is that law school outlines are significantly more intense and detailed.

How do you begin? First, set up your outline exactly according to the professor's syllabus. If he or she begins with "Jurisdiction" (as might happen in Civ Pro) then your outline should do the same. In fact, some syllabi contain a list of every case that is to be briefed for class – follow these in the order they are listed.

Next, define the topic (in this case, jurisdiction). You take a piece from your class notes, add a bit from your case notes and briefs, and then go ahead and stick in the entire summary from Black's Law Dictionary (which, if you remember, is your "Bible"). Then, list any and all elements that define the terms (more common in Contracts and Torts), and apply related, specific cases (again, following your syllabus, class notes, case notes, and briefs). Simple, right?

Note that every class, and every professor, is different so you have serious tailoring to do, but as a general rule, include case names and rules of law. Some professors don't care which case the rule came from, as long as you know what the rule is. Others make you know the rule and require you to also cite the case name that the rule of law comes from.

"Rules of law," are the courts' decisions from a case which become law as a result of the court ruling. As you may recall from prior vignettes, elements are almost mathematical. But don't worry – you don't have to major in math or accounting to understand them. You will use elements most heavily in classes like Torts, Criminal Law, and Contracts. They are lists of conditions which must be met and present to establish a charge. For example, the elements of a civil battery (not to be confused with "criminal battery") are: (1) an intent to commit a harmful or offensive contact to another person; and (2) an actual contact occurs resulting in some kind of injury to the person.

Things get a little confusing when you are looking for the first time at the big picture and are trying to piece that puzzle together. A criminal battery is basically any unwanted contact, just like the tort. However, criminal law is different from civil law. This confused me at first. Here's an easy way to know whether you are dealing with a crime or a tort. If the plaintiff is the State, you're dealing with a crime. In this case, the defendant will be found either innocent or guilty, and the State determines the punishment (*i.e.*, how much jail time). If, on the other hand, the plaintiff is a person, you're in the civil world. A battery charge would be for monetary compensation, so punishment would be money in my pocket to make me feel better for the black eye you gave me, rather than you going to jail.

"But wait," you say. "I've seen Law & Order and I know that you can't be punished twice for the same crime." Well, what you're referring to is a concept is called "double jeopardy," and no, it has nothing to do with Alex Trebek. It is a legal maxim that states a person can't be tried twice for the same crime. In our battery example, the person is not being tried twice for the same crime, because a criminal trial determines guilt or innocence and the civil case is about liability and, you guessed it, money (not justice).

I digress. The point is, you need to include all the elements for each tort (or crime or whatever) in your outline. You must know these! On exam day you're going to read a long, very detailed and confusing hypothetical. If you conclude there is a battery involved, you better be able to define exactly what a battery is and why or why not you think one is present.[29] You basically take the facts that the professor has given and say, "Well, Billy Joel had the intent to strike Tommy Lee because he told him if he called him Justin Bieber one more time he'd bash his head in with a stick, and he actually did bash his head in with the stick once he called him Justin Bieber that second time. In this case, intent was present, and a harmful contact to the victim did occur. Therefore the elements of a criminal battery are satisfied." Final grade = A+

Basically, your outlines summarize everything. Every damn thing you learned in every class. It won't be helpful if you study by just reviewing all your notes and all your briefs separately. You're better off outlining. Get everything shoved into one single, gigantic document. Then memorize it.

You could easily end up with seven hundred pages if you keep everything separate. Your outline on the other hand, may come to thirty or forty pages. Your call. Plus, the process of outlining unavoidably involves reviewing all those hundreds of pages anyway, so you're really getting most of your studying done just by creating the outline. Then memorize it.

The next step is revising your outline. After you go through it twenty or thirty times and talk it over with your study group, you knock out whatever sections you think are unnecessary, and the outline becomes over more concise. The more you review, the more concise it becomes. Eventually, and hopefully, you'll end up

---

29 Most likely, the exam hypo will involve multiple issues, plaintiffs, and defendants; be prepared for a very confusing hypo that will leave you feeling like you got hit by a train. And by the way, if you were hit by a train, who would you sue? [Note: if you even try to answer that question, then you are indeed starting to think like a lawyer!]

with a ten or fifteen page document that you know like the back of your hand.

Right before the exam, you won't have time, desire, or energy to study hundreds of pages of material. Ten or fifteen pages...maybe, but definitely no more. Outlining is how you actually learn the material. It puts everything together and into context by removing all the unnecessary grey matter. You write down everything, then condense, then memorize, then condense again, and so on, and so on. Continue this cycle as much as you can before you freak out and can't stand to look at the damn thing any more. At that point, you're ready.

But don't get too excited once you get to that point. Just because you successfully memorized all your outlines, doesn't mean all your notes were correct. An outline is only as good as the person who wrote it. So if you scam an outline off of an upper classman – like every good slacker should do – make sure to ask what grade that person got. An outline from a D student is worth just that. If you are going to scam, choose wisely.

The people who do the best are usually the ones hesitant to share. They don't want to give you, a slacker, the benefit of their hard work. So pretend to be their friend, buy 'em a few beers, sleep with them, whatever it takes just get the "A" student's outline. Remember your grades are the most important thing you have in this life.

<u>VOICE FROM THE FUTURE:</u> Get a few "upperclassmen" outlines only to see how they are set up. Get the form down, then throw them out. Do the work yourself. That is the only sure way you will learn.

23

A Brief Musical Interlude

♩♫♫♫♫♫♫♫♫♫♫♫♫♫♫♫♫♫♫

**Law School: The Musical,
Scene 5: "Torts"**

Main character slowly and wearily walks into a busy classroom and takes a seat in the last row. He hasn't slept in 36 hours (second time this week), exchanging sleep for time to work on a Legal Writing assignment that's due in two days. He didn't even have time to finish the assigned reading for the class in which he is now sitting. He also forgets to bring his glasses to class. As he rubs his head and eyes, he can barely make out the words "Torts I" on the chalkboard.

A few moments later the class begins. He does his best to pay attention, trying hard to focus on the case that is being discussed, however, sleep deprivation overtakes him, and his face sinks into his folded arms as he falls into a dream.

(Among the howls and laughter in the small corner of the bar where sat all the middle-aged lawyer men, their crazed antics are interrupted by a somber moment of truth when one of them opens his heart to his friends.)

Attorney #1:   Yea that's right boys, I got the sonuvabitch insurance company to settle on the Redman case. HA, HA, HA.

Attorney #2:   The Redman case? Isn't that the one where the scumbag guy sued that massage parlor for gross negligence?

Attorney #1:   That's right . . . the poor bastard was rendered completely impotent after that freak incident.

Attorney #3:   But I thought you told me that guy didn't have a chance in Hell of winning, because of that P.I. who took pictures of him a month later with that hooker in the motel?

Attorney #1:   Yea, but now the P.I. works for me . . . and I was so convincing in negotiations with my take on the Palsgraf and the "zone of danger" argument, that their insurance company got scared to death and decided to settle. Now I'm sitting on 33% of what my wonderful client will get, plus expenses! Isn't life grand! Come on boys, let's sing. Barkeep bring another round!

(The first attorney nods his head to the piano player, who winks back and begins to play their usual song. The first attorney then clears his voice and embraces the man next to him as they all burst out in perfect harmony.)

Chorus: Torts, Torts, Torts HOURRAY!
One, two and three cheers for Torts.

A Brief Musical Interlude

Verse 1:   No, an ambulance chaser is really no dork,
He's just an attorney who did well in Torts.
If you ever are injured, don't walk boy... run!
And sue 'em in Torts, it's a hellavulotta fun

Chorus: Torts, Torts, Torts HOURRAY!
One, two and three cheers for Torts

Verse 2:   Pay off your car loan, your house... AND MINE
Sue 'em in Torts and we'll all be just fine
Whether you been struck by car, bus or truck
If it was on purpose, or just by bad luck
Whether by bat, hat or a some guy named Matt
Or even by a girl who is ugly and fat
Sue everybody!

Chorus: Torts, Torts, Torts HOURRAY!
One, two and three cheers for Torts

Verse 3:   Whether the golf ball just barely missed
Or if he was right on the money with closed fist
If ever a case of simple hit and run
Sue 'em in Torts, it's a hellavulotta fun

Chorus: Torts, Torts, Torts HOURRAY!
One, two and three cheers for Torts

Verse 4:   If it's big money you want for pain you've been caused
When "victim" is all that you want to be called
Sue 'em in Torts, it's a hellavulotta fun
Yea, sue 'em in Torts and then bask in the sun

(They all carry the last word of the song out to perfection. They sound exactly like a well-rehearsed Barbershop Quartet. They are practiced and skilled. The entire Bar breaks out into applause for these wonderful entertainers and humanitarians. The bartender drops their drinks in front of them and tells them "this one's on me boys . . . thanks for the song." Even the piano player is clapping his hands off. What a glorious day.)

Main character awakes to sounds of clapping and laughter. He struggles momentarily to ascertain what is going on, and then suddenly realizes that all eyes are upon him. The room quickly draws silent, however, as an ominous figure begins lurching toward him until he reaches his desk, places both hands upon it, and slowly moves his face within inches of the now petrified One-L. "Go sleep somewhere else . . . You're outta here!" said the professor in a methodically calm, controlled, deep, and threatening voice.

Frightened and exceptionally embarrassed, the One-L quickly gathers his books and leaves the classroom. Sounds of laughter fill his ears as he shuts the door and drops his head in defeat. Seconds later, the laughter ends abruptly upon the booming sound of the professor's voice screaming out "QUIET!" As the class resumes, the One-L sinks to the floor and does his best to hold back his tears . . . although he's defeated in that endeavor as well.

END NOTES:
Palsgraf v. Long Island Railroad Co., 249 N.Y. 511, 164 N.E. 564, (N.Y. 1928), is a historic case by an infamous judge named Cardoza. The case involved a railroad employee who was helping a guy carrying a package onto a train. The passenger got on the train, but his package fell. The package was full of fireworks and exploded, causing an injury to Mrs. Palsgraf standing some distance away, who was silently waiting for her train to arrive. The

decision of the court was that in order to recover damages for the injury, Mrs. Palsgraf had to show that she was within the "Zone of Danger." The long and short of it is that since Mrs. Palsgraf couldn't show that the train attendants owed her a duty of care and that the accident was not foreseeable, she could not recover.

24

High School Revisited

The "Jerky Boys" were a trio of first-year students who all lived on campus and always hung out together. Their leader was given the nickname "Forrest," behind his back at first, to connect him to the mentally challenged fictitious character, Forrest Gump, whom some felt was his intellectual equal.

Let me tell you how the Jerky Boys[30] got their collective name. I have a couple of "Jerky Boys" albums (mind you, the original ones; not the censored mass media, politically correct versions you might find on sale today) which I occasionally play for friends. They are offensive but have good shock value to them and usually generate a laugh even from the most conservative of listeners. So I played a few tracks for the aforementioned trio, and they thought it was the funniest thing they had ever heard. Ever.

They began to quote the Jerky Boys incessantly. They began to implement certain coined phrases into their everyday vocabu-

---

30 The "Jerky Boys" were a NY trio who made and recorded prank phone calls with elaborate stories and ridiculously offensive characters. High humor for the unsophisticated crowd of the late 80s. I bought everything they sold.

lary. Their favorite phrase was, of course, "Sue Everybody!" So picture the three of them walking around together and anytime anything law related entered the discussion they inevitably interjected with the irrebuttable, "Sue Everybody!" The new Jerky Boys hung out together 24/7.

When we (the people who live on campus) first got to law school, groups formed quickly and mirrored those same cliques that existed in high school. All the cool guys and gals in one group; all the nerds in another. The jocks really didn't have their own group because there really are no jocks in law school,[31] seeing as how we don't have a law school football team, so any individuals who would normally be in the jock group mixed with the cool group. Of all the sixty or so students who lived on campus, there emerged about six distinct groups; ours was one of them. We were a "cool" group . . . kinda.

Each group experienced their own schisms in the first few months of school. The ones who were not cool enough were expelled from the cool groups, and others who were "too cool" slowly detached themselves from what they came to perceive as a "nerd group." No shit kids. Law school is just like high school. Every group eats at the crapateria at the same time and at the same table. They study together, play sports together and do whatever it is that the nerd group does (just joking here). On top of that they hang out together when they are sick of studying.

My group began to show its first signs of breakage when the Jerky Boys started to go solo. This trio could easily have been a quartet. As I was the source of the material and the defacto expert on same, I was considered one of the "Boys." To be tuthful, the

---

31 Present company excluded, of course.

members were all my friends, but in time, our original group lost some of its tightness.

Some of us did not eat at the same time, or did not invite everybody to play sports, or just avoided hanging out by claiming that they needed more study time. Disputes arose over who liked who and who was arrogant and who was a spoiled rich bastard, etc. Some hard feelings began to develop and the lines were drawn.

So my group split into two: The Jerky Boys went left and the rest went straight ahead. Where was I? I was on the fence. Granted, no one was physically threatening or fighting anyone else, but both sides often spoke of "taking" their former comrades. What's funny is that everybody, with one exception, actually discussed who they could beat up from the other group. I'm not kidding. Grown men actually spending time, a lot of time, discussing in earnest who would win in a fight.

You may wonder why I didn't I want to be a Jerky Boy. It's simply because the high school bullshit emanating from every pore of the collective jerky boy body was too much for me, so I had to figure out how to diplomatically move on.

One of the Jerky Boy, "Boots,"[32] loved to drink. He was not an alcoholic, but did get trashed whenever he went out. I was in fact rather shocked to find that a number of law students study their asses off during the week just so they can go out Friday night, get absolutely dead drunk, and recover by Monday. For them it's a way to release their law school student anger and frustration. A

---

32 This fine, young man's nickname was given to him because of the green construction boots he insisted on wearing with shorts. It didn't matter the type of shorts, khaki, dressy, jean shorts, work out shorts – whatever it was, he was wearing those green boots. Hard to avoid that nickname under the circumstances.

way to escape.

Another member of the Jerky Boy Clan was "KJ." This fellow was hardly a tag-along to his counterparts, and probably for this reason, it was likely he'd soon be banished from the Brotherhood. It was an all or nothing clan. KJ was on the outs with the Boys because, while he loved their attitude, he still felt awkward adopting their exact manners. I thought he was a bit too mature for their game. He loved using the coined phrases, but didn't like the over exaggeration or drinking. What a loser.

It was clear that KJ's main goal was achieving as much as he could in school. He, too, had chosen to sacrifice his lust for life for Civ Pro death. KJ's motivation for doing well was not just to get his diploma, but it was also to transfer out. KJ came from California, but did not get into any schools near home. His goal here in Florida was to be at the top of the class and transfer to a school back home.

Keep reading and you'll find out if he made it.

25

Jerky Boy 3, Open Memo Results and The End of Regular Classes

We've finally reached the red zone; the closing end of the first semester. The interesting thing is that in the last two weeks of classes most of the professors have flown through more material than they covered in the preceding 90% of the semester. That, my friends, is typical. Professors have syllabi and they want to cover it. Even if that means zooming through twelve topics a day when they normally cover two. And if you can't understand it, well that's too bad.[33] Classes are ending, and every professor is pounding out material. It's a ton of work.

To add to this chaos, we finally got back our open memo results from Legal Writing. Hurrah! Yours truly did very well. I ended up with the fourth highest grade in the class. Now recall that when the assignment came out, certain individuals chose to "collaborate." Here's how that played out:

When the results came back, those who worked together

---

33. In the professor's opinion.

ended up with different grades and as a result they immediately lost trust in each other. The inevitable question became, "if we used the exact same cases, how did you get a better grade than me?" Accusations of deceit, "holding back," and "chincing"[34] were liberally thrown around. The situation was so intense that a fist fight seemed to be the only way it was going to be resolved. Oh, you Jerky Boys!

Turns out KJ got the highest grade in his group. He, of course, worked "illegally" apart from the other two Jerky Boys. They worked together for days, sharing cases, arguing out issues, and constructing numerous outlines. How did one get a completely higher letter grade than the other? It turns out that what was in KJ's paper, and only KJ's paper, were in fact certain ideas which he did not "force" upon the group. Apparently, when they were discussing what issues and points should be included in their memos, KJ made a couple of offerings which the group thought were worthless. They dismissed KJ's points, but he decided to include and argue them in his own. The other "study partners" don't remember his offering these ideas. So, naturally, the others were absolutely pissed off and KJ was finally expelled from the group. "Benedict Arnold," became his new nickname to them. It was so bad that all they talked about was how they might beat the crap out of him and not get caught. The situation was tense, to say the least. On two separate occasions we had to hold them apart just for crossing paths.

Don't forget that study groups are all about trust. I share all my information with you and you share all your information with me. When the trust is broken and you get screwed, your grades

_____

34 Chincing, I think, means "you held out on me you sunovabitch!"

suffer. Remember that law school is competitive as Hell. Everybody wants to get to the top, and most people are willing to stab others in the back to get there. Maybe it's human nature.

Law school is all about class ranking. In KJ's situation, the higher he ranks, the better his chances are to transfer out of our school. In general, the higher you rank, the better your job potential, and therefore the more money you'll make. Which is why trusting your study group is so essential. The investment you make in your study group is really an investment in your future. I'll remind you again: choose well.

26

The Study Break

Every law school has a "Study Week" before exams. This occurs immediately following the end of regular classes, and you may have anywhere from three days to a week before your first exam depending on your schedule. During this time, you should prepare (or finish preparing) all outlines, and get ready to sit for exams. This is the time to refresh your memory, not to learn anything for the first time.

Our study week was only three days, not counting the weekend (which we had off anyway). Some work together on a chapter-by-chapter basis (meaning the whole group works on their outline to Chapter 1, then moves on together to Chapter 2), while others take the divide-and-conquer approach ("Billy, you take Chapter 1, Tommy, you take Chapter 2," and so on). Whichever you choose, keep in mind that this is the most important time of the semester. If you miss a critical point of the class in your outline and that point comes up in the exam… well, let's just say you're in bad shape.

This is undoubtedly a stressful time, and many people really start to freak out.[35]

Personally, I worked on my outlines alone and exchanged copies with my two study partners. It was simple. We got together once for a few hours to exchange and discuss our outlines and to clear up any confusing points we had. Recall that during the regular semester we would regularly call each other to ask questions, discuss major hurdles or just to argue some position. In preparing for exams, however, both the girls in my group and I felt we were better off working individually and conferring as necessary.

We were comfortable with the arrangement because we all went to class every day, briefed every case assigned, and really worked hard to understand the material. We were all smart and motivated, and really didn't need to depend on others. Our study group was tailored to our needs, and was thus, rather limited. And that was that. We got our work done, remained friends, and none of us got on each other's nerves. Other groups weren't as fortunate.

For example, the Jerky Boys, including the once-expelled KJ, who somehow managed to get back in the good graces of his previously betrayed comrades, and a new guy from their section, chose to create their outlines together. The new guy, who went by the call name of "Blue," [36] lived off campus. The Boys collected all their belongings (books, outlines, notes, portable computers, etc.) and went over to Blue's pad during Study Week. With that, the Jerky Boys disappeared from campus literally for days on end. It was a nice change for the rest of us. The dorms were calm and ac-

---

35 Surprised?

36 Perhaps because it was a primary color, I'm not sure.

tually study conducive for once. No door pounding. No annoying laughter. No pranks. Just peace.

Did this strategy work for the Boys? They went over every note, every case, and every rule over and over and over again. They would argue, review, argue, and review again. They basically beat the hell out of each other with knowledge. It was through this forceful repetition that they learned the material.

Their study strategy had its advantages. They definitely went through the material enough times to retain it, and each partner helped the other figure out unclear concepts. The main disadvantage, however, was that they spent major time with one another. Twenty-four hours a day for all five study days. They ate together, slept together, breathed together, studied together, and argued together the whole way through. Add the fact that Blue's apartment was small, coupled with the Boys' sophomoric antics, made it the perfect recipe for an explosion.

I wondered why the Boys decided to study with KJ after their troubled past. Apparently they forgave him (kinda) and felt that since they had done so much work together during the semester, they would all be better off finishing together. Big mistake.

Forrest, Boots, and Blue got the funny feeling that KJ was holding out on them again. They noticed that, at night, KJ would wake up, and furiously write in his notebook or silently type on his computer. KJ admitted to doing this, but insisted there was no dubious intention. He woke up every night because, he claimed, a thought would enter his mind and he wanted to make sure he got it on paper. The others weren't convinced. They accused him of repeat behavior – getting everything he could from the group and holding back his own ideas. KJ responded by offering to share all his written and typed notes. "Look through my desk, my computer files, my drawers! Take anything you want," he told them.

During Study Week, One-Ls are nervous as Hell, excitable, not sleeping well, eating poorly, and basically scared shitless. It was no wonder, adding KJ's previous betrayal to that mix with the possibility of that happening again, that the Boys went through all of KJ's notes. Even when no smoking gun was found, the accusations continued to fly. It got so bad that they were fighting more than they were studying. Then the inevitable "bomb" went off. Unconfirmed reports of violence spread and suddenly KJ was formally and officially out of the Jerky Boys. This time, they all swore, for good.

KJ was now drifting and groupless. The Jerky Boys hated him and there were really no other options for him. His reputation had been tarnished and even if there was enough time to join a new group and contribute, I doubt any group would have taken him in at that time – there was too much "possibility" that he was a snake. So that was it. KJ had to fly solo through the One-L exams from that point on.

27

A Brief Musical Interlude

Law School: The Musical, Scene 7: "Exams"

This scene takes place on a split stage, half showing the main gathering spot of the Law School outside of the library, the other half showing the dorms. Students are moving in and out of the areas at a frantic pace. In front of the library a few study groups are hotly debating the likely subject matter of their first exam. On the same side of the stage numerous students and faculty members flood in and out of the library and classrooms. On the second half of the stage, students race in and out of their tiny dorm rooms; others stand at the dormitory balcony and converse. All students are tired, nervous, and scared to death. Clearly the first semester is ending and all are preparing for final exams.

As the students race around like lost, starving rats, a few conversations are overheard by the audience. On the top balcony of the dorms, one student is enthusiastically attempting to convince another student how unfair it is that his entire grade for the semester is based on one, four-hour performance. "Come on man," says the student earnestly, "I've been killing myself for sixteen weeks and my entire grade is only based on how well I do on . . . one . . . single . . . test? That's just not fair man. It's the system man, it's just meant to keep us down." His fellow student nods his head in apathetic support and responds "I know dude, but what can we do about it? You think that the administration gives a rats ass about us students, hmph, not a chance."

In front of the library another duo are then overheard by the audience. Two well dressed young ladies are sitting quietly with looks of utter despair on their faces. The first confides in her study partner on how terrified she is about the upcoming exams. "I have never been so scared in my entire life," she says with a trembling voice. "I have five exams in twelve days, all closed book, how on earth am I ever going to memorize everything in time? I honestly have no idea how I am going to pass all these exams." The partner responds sarcastically, "You think that's bad, I still haven't figured out what Civ Pro is." A third-year student walking by hears this last comment and softly laughs. "Ah, One-L Life," he murmurs to himself.

Suddenly, two male students race by the study groups and professors, one chasing after the other. All eyes turn on the two as the predator leaps over a table and captures his slower prey. The predator then flips his captive onto its back and begins strangling him with fierce animosity. As his hands violently choke the prey, he screams out "Give me the outline now! You said I could have the outline! You promised! You promised damnit!" All eyes watch with the excitement for a few moments before a few Three-L students dive in and save the first-year student from what would surely have been his demise at the hands of his jilted study partner. Surprisingly enough, however, none of the students or faculty are shocked by the incident. It happens. People really freak out during Law School examinations.

Music then fills our ears as students on both sides of the stage join in the chorus.

Chorus: A powerful pressure pounds on our brains
(all students) As we read all our outlines again and again
              With only four hours to show all we know
              We're scared to death of this first-year talent show

              It might not be so bad if we could just comprehend
              What the Hell the professors want on their exams
              So we memorize everything as best as we can
              Oh God! How we're scared of these first-year exams

Main character's study group then takes center stage and begins the first verse.

Charlie: I've always kept my body and mind in top shape
(jock)   Thought I could handle anything that passed my way
              But this stress has driven my health to the dogs
              And I've started smoking a pack a day

Sheri: I love this rush, wish I could study more
(liberal)   Twenty-four-seven is perfect for me
              I study for twenty, and in the last four
              I listen to audio tapes while I sleep

Lisa: (attractive, quasi- intelligent)	I wish I could stay awake But sleep is too enticing for me to break free In fact, if I want to study at all I need Ginsing, vitamins, and ten cups of coffee
Jason: (dead-head)	What? Study all day . . . every day!? Sorry . . . I just don't have the time I need an escape from this Law School crap That's why I'm stoned all the time
Chorus: (all students)	A powerful pressure pounds on our brains As we read all our outlines again and again With only four hours to show all we know We're scared to death of this first-year talent show
	It might not be so bad if we could just comprehend What the Hell the professors want on their exams So we memorize everything as best as we can Oh God! How we're scared of these first-year exams

The second verse is then continued by a student in the dorms who is pacing back and forth in his room. His walls are covered with pages from his outlines and notes, and gigantic mnemonic devices are posted over his bed. One such mnemonic is clearly visible to all eyes; it reads: "Get Serious Most Contracts Don't Depend on 2 People." The student eyes this with total concentration and then begins.

Verse 2:	The G in "Get"is for the Gateway case The S is for Tober v. Skinner MC is for Modification of Contracts Oh . . . I think we have a winner!

A Brief Musical Interlude

"Don't Depend"is for Discharge of Duty
The 2 is U.C.C. section 2-209
The P in "People"represents Performance
Uhh . . . I'm never gonna come out of this test alive!

That's not bad, six hours well spent
But considering that I haven't even made a dent
I just won't sleep for these next twelve days
Just memorize and memorize and totally fry my brain

Chorus:	A powerful pressure pounds on our brains
(all students)	As we read all our outlines again and again
	With only four hours to show all we know
	We're scared to death of this first-year talent show

It might not be so bad if we could just comprehend
What the Hell the professors want on their exams
So we memorize everything as best as we can
Oh God! How we're scared of these first-year exams

Main Character then rises from the dorm room immediately adjacent to his "Mnemonic King" neighbor, and addresses the audience for the last verse.

Verse 3:	Yea, we're freaking out
	Would you expect any less
	Don't forget most of us are here
	To do our very best

God forbid we fail out
What would we do then
Cry, cry, cry and then go home

Not a very good plan

So we kill ourselves
Study as much as we can
And pray that we'll pass
Our first-year exams

Chorus: A powerful pressure pounds on our brains
(all students)   As we read all our outlines again and again
                 With only four hours to show all we know
                 We're scared to death of this first-year talent show

It might not be so bad if we could just comprehend
What the Hell the professors want on their exams
So we memorize everything as best as we can
Oh God! How we're scared of these first-year exams

END NOTES:

The "Gateway case" is formally known as Gateway Co. v. Charlotte Theatres, 297 F.2d 483(1st Cir. 1961). "Tober v. Skinner" is actually the case of Skinner v. Tober Foreign Motors, Inc., 345 Mass. 429, 187 N.E.2d 669 (1963). "U.C.C. § 2-209" refers to section 2 subsection 209 of the Uniform Commercial Code. This subsection specifically deals with Modification, Rescission and Waiver of Contracts. The Code is basically a set of rules that business are required to follow when entering into any transaction or sale.

28

People Freaking Out During Exams

As you have surely gathered by now, stress is a reoccurring theme in this Law School drama. And stress makes seemingly normal, in-control people, do wild things. For me, the best part of this psychological experiment was watching people escape from the pressure cooker by doing things you never thought they would do.

For example, when an outspoken, nonsmoker who regularly preaches the terrors of smoking, turns into a two-pack a day chimney, you know there's a little stress in his life. Similarly, if a four-hundred-pound man who has clearly never exercised a day in his life is suddenly out jogging at five o'clock in the morning, it's clear that he's a bit stressed out too. All of a sudden I'm a law school Jeff Foxworthy: "You may be a stressed law student if…"

Sleeping all day to avoid studying is another good indicator that stress has overcome you. Complete abstinence or sudden promiscuity are other signs. People average two to three hours of sleep a night. Throw in the smoking, the workouts, fights, sex, crying and related hysterics, and you are talking about a freaking zoo with open cages. It's wild.

There are a lot of great stories about people being absurdly affected by the stress of exams and the closing of the academic grading period. Let me now share an endearing exam-related stress story for your edification and enjoyment.

Surprisingly, stress affects even the most seasoned law school veterans: the Three-Ls. In this first story, a third-year student had a first-year roommate. Apparently the two already were not getting along so well because the One-L wasn't so good about washing his dishes and keeping their kitchen clean, so one day during Study Week, the Three-L, clearly stressed over exams, attacked and choked the One-L right outside the law library.

There are a lot of tables outside the library, and a lot of students sit out there between classes, smoking, socializing, and relaxing. On this particular day, stress got the better of Three-L, and he attacked his roommate for admitting that he did not clean the kitchen before he left for school. A Three-L friend told me that the breakdown had less to do with the state of cleanliness of his kitchen and more to do with the stress he was very poorly handling over a paper that was due. Regardless of the cause, it was pretty serious. Police were called, statements taken, the whole shabang.

I don't know if battery charges were filed by the victim, but as a One-L, I can tell you that all the elements of that crime were present. There was a harmful or offensive contact without the consent of the victim and there was an injury. Book e'm Dano.

You would think that a Three-L would have mastered stress management by now, but obviously not. If I needed proof that the stress level continues in years 2 and 3 of this Law School game, I needed it no more.

29

Examinations

Want to know what law school examinations are like? "Yeah?" Well, you came to the right place. Each exam is anywhere from three to four hours long. These are essay tests. No multiple choice. Just four, grueling hours of writing as fast as your little hand can go.

For One-Ls, there is no final exam in Legal Writing, so we only have four classes to prepare for: Contracts, Torts, Crim, and Civ Pro. The style and content of all the exams are similar: a hypothetical scenario for you to analyze.

You start with some crazy story and end with a nice open-ended question (or questions) for you to answer. Allow me to provide you with an example:

HYPO

Joe was walking down the street with his new Beats by Dr. Dre™ blasting out the soundtrack of *Yentle,* when he negligently failed to look both ways before he crossed.

Paul left his house after his parents had told him several times that his tires were absolutely low on air and that he should fill them up before he caused an accident. Paul was driving down the road when one of his tires blew out. The car spun and struck Joe as he was about to belt out the harmony of the chorus to "Papa, Can You Hear Me?" Paul was unhurt by the collision, but his car was damaged. Joe was knocked unconscious and lay still on the ground bleeding. Paul immediately saw the blood and knew Joe was hurt badly. Paul looked across the street and saw a payphone. Paul reached into his pocket and felt the jingling of change - clearly enough for a phone call. Instead of phoning for an ambulance, Paul opened his trunk, pulled out a spare tire, and changed the one that blew. When he was done, twenty-two minutes later, Paul got into his car and drove to the nearest hospital, where he told them what had happened. The hospital team immediately took off and picked up Joe, who by then was much worse. At the hospital, Joe received emergency care but was only given a sixty-five percent chance to live. However, the doctors mixed up the files and Joe was given the wrong medication and died.

The question given by the prof for the above hypothetical scenario would be something like: Discuss the remedies, liabilities, and legal consequences for all parties involved.

Real exam hypos are usually about five or six pages long. What I gave you was about half a page. So a four-hour exam is barely enough time to finish writing . . . if you write like a demon.

So how do you answer a question like this? You describe why Paul was negligent, why Joe was negligent, why the hospital was negligent, and who was most responsible for the death. You should also point out that Joe has no cause of action – no ability to sue in a civil action for monetary damages, because he is dead, but his family or estate can. A dead person has no standing (pun intended) to sue in a civil action. So in your essay you go through all the information locked up in your head and slap it all down on paper – every potential cause of action with its corresponding list of elements. You explain if every element is satisfied and lay out every idea you have. All of it. The professors want to see how well you explain your knowledge of the law to them in a short amount of time.

The most popular method used in answering these types of hypotheticals is called "I.R.A.C." That's: Issue, Rule of Law, Analysis, and Conclusion. Name the first Issue you are going to talk about: Joe's negligence in failing to look both ways before crossing the street. Analyze and explain it. You create a paragraph wherein every issue you find is discussed. First you identify your Issue, then you state the Rule of Law, make your Analysis, then wrap it all up in your Conclusion.

Then you go to your next paragraph and do the same thing for your second issue: Paul's negligence in not filling his tires up with air. The order of your issues doesn't matter as long as you get them all in. You could start with Paul's assault on Joe, or with the hospital's negligence (and the specific nurses and doctors involved) in giving Joe the wrong meds. Whatever you want, but I would start with the most important ones that will give you the most points.

When you are writing about the Rule of Law you are showing the prof that you know the exact elements necessary to prove the cause of action you are addressing. For example here is what you should write in this part: "Negligence requires that the actor has a duty to the victim, that that duty was breached by the actor, that the breach of that duty caused the injury, and that the victim was damaged (injured) as a result." This tells the prof that you know all the elements of the tort.

In the Analysis part, you are discussing each of the elements individually. So, first, you would make a determination as to whether Joe actually had a duty to look both ways before crossing the street. All you need is common sense to answer this question. I would say that unless Joe violated some other law, like jay-walking, or crossing the street on a red light, then he had no duty to look both ways. Children are taught to look both ways to protect them from harm, but there really is no duty to look both ways.

A "red herring" that you want to avoid in this HYPO is posing and then answering any question about whether Joe crossed at a red light or jay-walked, because the facts presented do not include this information – so don't make them up. For all we know, Joe may have been walking through a painted crosswalk with a green light. So you provide answers based on what you know. It seems that in this case our analysis need go no further. Because we can't prove that Joe had a duty, we can't prove that he was negligent. You need to prove every element to establish the tort. If we could establish that Joe did have a duty, then we would have to discuss whether Joe breached that duty. If we wanted to make up a law for argument's sake which says that Joe had to look both ways before crossing the street because of the new Florida statutes passed that forces people whose names begin with "J" to look both ways before crossing any street, and he did not do this. . . the second condition of breach is established. (Note that when using a specific law, unless the prof names it, you need to tell him where you got it from. This is called in legalese: citing to authority). If I'm using a rule of law from a Supreme Court case, I'll need to tell the prof what case I got it from.

The next element you would need to address is whether Joe's breach caused the accident. "If Joe had not broken the law and looked both ways, he would have seen Paul's tire blow out and would not have been in the middle of the street when the car went out of control, and thus would never have been hurt in the first place."

Finally, to satisfy the last element, you show that Joe was actually injured, which should be obvious by the fact that he died at the end of the HYPO... but if you don't write in your answer that this element was satisfied by his death, then you don't get any points for it.

I hope you didn't get confused by this statement in the hypo: "Joe negligently failed to look both ways before crossing the street." Just because a prof includes the word "negligent" doesn't mean that the person was actually negligent in a court of law. Joe didn't look both ways, but as far as our analysis is concerned, he didn't have to.

Now we have reached the Conclusion. The trick here is that you don't conclude anything. You don't write "Joe was not negligent." What you write is more like: "Under the facts presented to us, it seems that Joe was not negligent in that he had no duty to look both ways before crossing the street. Had the facts provided us with more information about whether he crossed the street illegally (e.g., through a red light or by jay-walking) then perhaps a duty might have been established.

That was one simple I.R.A.C.! FYI: in the half-page hypo I

set up for you there are eight or so separate issues that need to be dissected, analyzed and explained. We just did one here. That means seven more I.R.A.C.s. For all you over-achievers out there: happy hunting!

To conclude this section, as you will come to realize when really getting your hands into this, doing very well in an exam requires you to know the "law" for your class (the "elements" in the Torts example above), and to be able to very quickly analyze a fact pattern to determine every possible cause of action, then write intelligently and cohesively how the facts apply to the law. And when I say, "quickly," I am not joking. Pages and pages and pages of hand-written analysis are what you are going to turn in. So you must have legible handwriting and be able to write like the wind. No joke. Start practicing now.

30

More Exam Tips

What else do you need to know about exams? You need to know about supplemental study aids. These are case notes and other materials you can purchase which summarize classes for you. There are also audiotapes from renowned professors who explain courses in simpler terms than your professors. Additionally, there are books which summarize and simplify your classes, such as a Hornbook, a Nutshell, a Blonde's or Glannon.

The moral majority at our law school deem this sort of material evil. "You shouldn't use this material . . . you don't need it . . . you can learn this material on your own . . . your own outline is all you need to succeed." And "if we catch you using it, you're going to be punished." That's basically the schpiel the professors and deans use to get students to avoid even looking at this corrupting and offensive material. It's ironic, however, that every bookstore of every law school sells these supplements… and they sell a lot of them.

The truth is that the administration knows you're using these books; they probably used the same ones when they were in school. And they know that most students need this material to understand what is going on in most courses. What they don't want you to do is rely on this material so much that you can't brief or understand a case on your own. They want you to actually do the work.

Slackers are definitely the first to buy supplements, but the majority of students eventually pick up one or two for the classes they are having a hard time with. If you do decide to get a supplement, don't stop reading and briefing cases. Use these books the right way, to help make the process a little easier. You will, inevitably, have to brief horrific, thirty-page cases which, after three hours of reading and analyzing, will still make no sense to you. For a complicated case like that, it makes perfect sense to use a supplement to see its synopsis and analysis. It can help you identify the issues, rules of law, and other significant information.[37] Once you've done that, review the case. I bet ten-to-one you'll understand it.

Law school is packed with work. You will always be busy, so use whatever you can to make it more manageable.

Here are some other helpful exam-journey tips:

1. Preparation really does pay off. If you study hard during the semester, you won't have to spend critical study break time "learning." Rather, you'll just be reviewing.

---

37 Many cases include a lot of "dicta" which seems important because it's written by a judge, but isn't actually part of the holding. Dicta are the judge's opinions on something, though he/she doesn't directly rely on them to come to the legal conclusion. While dicta are informative, they arearen't critical to understanding case law, and often just confuse and overwhelm students.

2. If you're ready, you won't need to cram the night before.

Don't pull an all-nighter. Even if you're not fully prepared don't do it. This is not high school or undergrad; these exams are cumulative.

3. If you don't know the material by the night before, the best thing you can do is get a good night's sleep so you can bullshit your way through the exam with a clear head. If you stay up all night before a four hour exam, you probably won't be sharp and you won't write well. The night before an exam you should RELAX. I, personally like to read poetry. Before every exam I would read the following poems in the following or der: Eliot's "The Lovesong of J. Alfred Prufrock"; Cavafy's "Waiting for the Barbarians" and "One Night." Then I would read Samuel Talor Coleridge's "Kubla Kahn" and Eugene Field's "Little Boy Blue." Then I would do my best to read out loud Poe's "The Bells" without making any mistakes and wrap up with Kipling's "If." But everyone is different. Maybe you want to play some Zombie Apocalypse video game or play Solitare; maybe you want to take a five-mile run; maybe you just want to get a massage. Whatever you choose, just remember to RELAX.

4. Get to bed early, and if you have an afternoon exam, sleep in.

31

Post-Exam Blowout (Or is it Blow Up?)

The day has finally come. I just took my last exam, and I am DONE! Yahoo!

They say in law school, if you can make it through your first semester, you can make it through all three years. I think I just made it through my first semester, so I can almost taste the graduation cake.

As soon as we – the Jerky Boys and the Geeks – finished, we agreed to all go out and party together. Finishing your round of exams is such a rush, we were all in the "Why Not?!" mentality.

It was just supposed to be a fun night. Just a bunch of guys going out to celebrate, but the reality was that we were tired. Very tired. No, more than that. We were overworked, exhausted, and drained of spirit. Those last few weeks of school were filled with wave after wave of pressure and more pressure. The only thing we had to look forward to in our miserable lives was this "Post-Exam Blowout." So now that we were actually on our way to the bar to celebrate, we pushed aside our exhaustion and did our best to relax. This was, of course, easier said than done.

We went to a local bar, and though I wouldn't know it because I had only gone out twice during the semester and had never been there, it was apparently the law school students' favorite hangout. Not surprisingly, it was packed with law school students, all in equal celebration mode.

For me at least, I was looking forward to a simple night of laughing, drinking, and just being a little loud. I thought everyone else would be of the same mindset. I did not anticipate the explosions of post-war anxiety that revealed just how stressed we really were. We were never taught the elements for Post Traumatic Stress Disorder, but I'm sure every element was satisfied.

The night quickly became a heavyweight championship fight.

"Ladies and gentlemen, welcome to tonight's main event. Before the fighters enter the ring and throw their first punches, let's tell you a little about each of them."

-------------- PRE-FIGHT --------------

One young lady who we called "Lizard," because she was a snake and scammed outlines from anybody she could, was already there... and drunk. She was a mean drunk, too: nice on the outside, bitch on the inside. One of my friends, Dylan, slept with her during the semester, and subsequently blew her off. This, of course, she didn't appreciate.

We knew as soon as we saw her standing there drunk and loud that the situation was volatile. We did our best to avoid her, and though the bar was big, it wasn't that big. We played darts and drank; we laughed and hung out; we mingled and socialized.

Then we noticed Lizard crying. She was sitting at the bar, talking with a classmate called "Bull." He was a snake, too. But Bull didn't snake outlines, he drank, and tried to sleep with every woman in our class. "A" for effort. "F" for results. We couldn't help but laugh as Bull consoled Lizard. A vulnerable girl was his dream date.

I don't know if it was because of all the brews I had consumed, or if it was because I just had a sick sense of wonder, but I approached the two and asked how they were doing. Lizard was crying and wiping her eyes continuously. I tried a quick exit move to go to the restroom, but Liz grabbed me by the arm and said, "Do you know what this man just said to me?" referring to Bull. "He told me that I was the most beautiful woman he'd ever seen and that he'd love to spend the night with me."

I almost blew my head off with laughter. I looked at Bull to see his reaction. He sat there, looking as if someone had just shot his dog. The poor bastard. I couldn't help but feel sorry for him.

Then from the corner of her eye, Liz saw Dylan hitting on a young lady and seemingly doing a good job at it because the girl was laughing and it looked like they were enjoying themselves. Lizard apparently had seen enough. She slithered to our table and pulled up a chair. The Bull followed quietly behind her... just waiting....

"The fighters have entered the ring, ladies and gentlemen. Sound the bell and let the first round begin!" Ding, Ding.

---------------- ROUND 1 ----------------

There were about ten of us at the table, including Liz and the Bull. Unfortunately, nobody questioned their joining us or asked them to leave. Dylan noticed Liz, and shook his head at me as if to say "What the hell is she doing here?" I knew, though didn't verbalize the answer: making trouble. To divert my attention, I started talking to a fellow classmate of mine.

Some time passed. The guys were still talking to their girls, I was talking to some friends, and Liz was pounding down the beers, mumbling to Bull, and staring at Dylan with eyes full of daggers.

All of a sudden Liz yelled out, "Don't believe a fucking word out of his mouth!" Everyone's jaw dropped.

"Oh my God," one of the girls said as her jaw dropped.

"Oh, shit," I added.

Dylan looked over at her with an expression of absolute disgust and frustration. Lizard was going to ruin it for him. After a few seconds of silence, everyone started to resume their conversations (even Dylan and his new friend). But that just fueled Liz on.

A minute or so later she did the same thing, this time almost falling out of her chair while screaming, "He's a fucking liar . . . he's full of shit." Again the same reaction from the crowd. I couldn't let her do this to my buddy (I am loyal to fault), so I went over and grabbed her by the arm, and told her I wanted to talk to her. She went with me without any struggle.

I took her to the bar and bought her a Coke. The first thing out of her mouth was, "Mike . . . why won't you just save me from all these assholes?" Oh, what did I get myself into?

-------------- ROUND 2 --------------

Meanwhile at the table, things were getting wild. Another classmate, whom everyone hated, was sitting a few chairs away. It was a sad irony that nobody liked her, because she certainly seemed to like everyone. Everyone, that is, but KJ. I don't know why, but she hated him even though they never really talked to one another. Maybe he reminded her of an old boyfriend; who knows?

With no warning at all, she leapt out of her chair and started SCREAMING at KJ. No shit – SCREAMING!!!

"You are the biggest liar I have ever seen in my life. All you do is go around telling your lies and sticking your nose in everybody else's business. You're a fucking asshole!"

Everybody in the bar turned to look.

Fine representatives of our school, I thought to myself.

"What the hell are you talking about?" KJ yelled back.

"You know exactly what I'm talking about, you sonofabitch ... exactly!" she coldly responded.

What a night.   In a word: drama! This was not my idea of relaxing.

---------------- FINAL SCORECARD ----------------

That night, Liz ended up going home alone, sorry Bull. KJ also went home alone. My buddies went out to some club to go dancing with their new friends. A few other classmates ended up spending the night with other classmates and the gossip, of course, spread like wildfire. I went home and went to bed – enough drama for me.

"And that, ladies and gentlemen was the main event. We hoped you enjoyed the show."

32

Moving Out

I don't know if I'm happier to be finished with exams or to be moving out of the dorms. And you know what, who cares? Today is a glorious day because I am done with dorms forever.

I moved into a small apartment with "Data," a computer whiz friend of mine. The rent was high, but that was a small price to pay to get out of the high school, powder keg, gossip plagued, drama, drama, drama that was life in the dorms.

Hopefully next semester I will have some semblance of normalcy in my life. I wouldn't be on campus all the time. Always at school. Always thinking about school. School, school, school! With this move I hope to have a little separation, a little escape. I would still have all the homework, but at least I'd be doing the work somewhere other than in the library or in my crazy dorm.

In that sense it was very exciting and liberating. The only downside was that when I did need to go the library, make a copy, print some notes, or see a professor, I'd have to get in my car and drive fifteen minutes instead of taking a five-minute walk. Small price to pay.

I hoped it would work because Data seemed like a nice guy. Then again, I thought, he must have had a personality disorder or he wouldn't be in law school to begin with, so I guess I would find out soon enough. Our personalities seemed to mesh, so I hoped we wouldn't have many, if any, arguments or confrontations. He was not a Joe Cool, but who is in law school?[38] He was a hard-working student, well mannered, and non-deviant (I hoped).

He was a better choice than either of the Jerky Boys for obvious reasons: he is a studier, not a partier. Let me end here by repeating the words of a wizened, Buddhist monk who said "you never know, until you know."

---

38 Except for me, of course.

33

Grades and the Metamorphasis So Far

Drum roll please . . . tap, tap, tap, tap, tap, tap, tap, tap, tap, tap, tap, tap.

The envelope in my hands, I paused and cradled it as if it were a letter from a long lost lover. It was as if I were opening a letter that contained the answer to the mysteries of life and death. A sacred text with ancient secrets etched in gold. I trembled slightly as I ripped the perforated edges, heaving a deep sigh in anticipation. A sigh that exhaled with it all my doubts, worries, and fears.

I saw an "A." Good start. Oooh damn, I also saw a "C." I saw a "B." I saw a "B+" under that, and a "B-" under that. Ouch! I had hoped for a little better. At least I got an "A" in Legal Writing. I was happy with that. I got a "B" in torts. That was pretty good. Civ Pro? Well . . . I guess I deserved a C. I really didn't know what was going on in that class. "B+" in Crim, which was better than I thought I'd get. But, ouch… I got a "B-" in Contracts. That hurt. I thought I really understood that class. I thought I killed that exam. I never missed a class, briefed every case, and studied for it like mad. But after I thought for a few minutes and recalled that the professor told us that he had given out 27 Ds and Fs the previous year, and that he didn't care because he had tenure and couldn't be fired, I guess a "B-" wasn't so bad.

Opening that envelope and seeing those grades was extremely anticlimactic. There was so much anticipation, so many hopes, and so much excitement, that it was actually a let down. My peers, on average, did about the same as me.

At our school, a student who made Dean's List received a $3,000 tuition cut. For some students, including me, that was a huge chunk of change.

To be honest, I was just happy I didn't get less than a 2.0. If that happened, you ended up on probation. About thirty students – 15 percent of the class – did and were put on probation and had to take a remedial course to teach them how to be better law students. Glad I wasn't there but I vowed to focus more over the next two and a half years. Remembering my father's words, I was going to give it my best, and hopefully bring up my GPA.

I asked a few upperclassmen their opinions on how well I did grade-wise. Most of them said I did extremely well and not one said that I dropped the ball. Those I asked said that my GPA should place me in the top third of the class. I would, of course have liked to be in the top quarter or top ten, but top third was not bad either. So it was pretty good start after all.

One upperclassman confided in me that he was on academic probation his first semester, but by the end of his second year he had climbed up to the top third of the class. So he went from the bottom to the top third. How? He told me that after the first year the profs started grading more in accordance with what you should get. The first year profs intentionally tried to screw you in grading, because it was the school's policy to flunk out twenty percent of the class. Well, it turned out that this info was correct because one quarter of my section was on probation. I guess that put my first semester grades into perspective.

After only one semester of law school, I noticed big changes in myself. Most significantly, I developed a professional attitude. I'd never been so dedicated to something as I was to law school. And I had to be, just to make it. I had to study every day, practically all day every day to get through, but I did it! I finished my first semester. I found something within myself, something deep down, and although I bitched about the work the whole way through, just like everybody else, I'd had my first taste of success and I actually felt like I belonged here. Like I was smart enough to do this and that I was going to do this!

34

Second Semester Classes and Schedule

The second semester begins! My classes included: Torts 2 (the second half of the Torts class); Civ Pro 2 (same Part II class); Contracts 2 (ditto); Appellate Advocacy (you guessed it: the second legal writing class); and Property (wake up, that's a new class!).

First year classes are pretty much the same no matter what law school you attend. So you should expect to take these classes in your first year: Contracts, Torts, Property, Criminal Law, Civil Procedure, Constitutional Law, probably two Legal Research and Writing courses, and maybe an International Law or Comparative Law class. These are the fundamental classes.

A big plus for me this semester was that my class schedule was absolutely awesome. On Mondays and Wednesdays I had an 11 a.m. and a 1 p.m., so I was out of there by 2:30 p.m. On Tuesdays and Thursdays I had a 9 a.m. and a 2 p.m. so I was out of there by 3:30 p.m. On Fridays I had no class! Yahoo!

Having no class on Friday was great because I could sleep in – always a good thing. Plus, now I had three days instead of two to do homework. Big difference! If I really put in the effort Fridays and Saturdays, then I could have Sundays "off." If I stuck with the plan, I could actually do something on the weekends – go to the beach, or go out with my friends at night, or go on a date, or watch a football game . . . you know, have a life!

This was going to work out great. My whole intention in moving off-campus was to have more time to socialize, and with this schedule my dream could become reality. Things were definitely going my way.

35

Appellate Brief From Hell

The huge Appellate Advocacy assignment was finally due. The hypothetical we were given was a case that had already gone through a jury trial and our assignment was to prepare the appeal.

The case involved a young guy who had been challenged to a "one on one" fight, but showed up at the fight with a shotgun, and shot his challenger. He lost the trial and was convicted of assault with a deadly weapon. Half the class prepared the prosecution (*i.e.*, worked for "the State" in trying to preserve the guilty verdict), and the other half acted on behalf of the defendant.

The "prosecutors" had to convince the appeals court that the conviction should be upheld while the "public defenders" (myself included) had to argue why the conviction should be overturned. We were given over two hundred pages of information detailing the incident, case history, and court activity, including the trial court transcripts.

The first issue was whether the voir dire (or, in English, the jury selection)[39] was properly conducted. During voir dire, either side may excuse prospective jurors either under the preemptory rule or "for cause." If an attorney doesn't think a potential juror should sit on the panel, for any nondiscriminatory reason, that attorney can peremptorily excuse the juror.[40] According to the hypo, the State was seemingly excusing prospective jurors because they were either women or African Americans.

It was up to the defense to find and research U.S. Supreme Court and/or Florida Supreme Court decisions which found these peremptory challenges discriminatory, and therefore not allowed.

Then the defense had to prove that discrimination actually took place. Most states have a pretty low standard, and as long as the excusing attorney can give any reason other than "she's a woman" or "he's black," the judge is unlikely to find discrimination. The hypo facts, of course, were ambiguous, so it was up to each person to prove his or her case.

The second issue on appeal was the fact that our client's feet were shackled and a bailiff stood by the stand "guarding him" one day during trial. The shackles could easily sway a juror into thinking the defendant was a "security risk." If any of them did perceive him as a threat, they might also think he was capable of committing the alleged crime. Our task again was to research, apply the facts of our case to the law we found, and make our best arguments in support of our client's position. We needed to show that the defendant, a college student with exemplary behavior while in custody, was not a security risk. What I argued was that the only reason he was shackled was due to court inefficiency and

---

39 And pronounced "vwaah deer."
40 Different states have different voire dire procedure. Florida, for example, allows each side (both the prosecutor and the defense) three peremptory challenges.

lack of security personnel. Therefore, I argued on appeal that he should never have been forced to wear the shackles, but because they made him do so and "guarded" him, the jury was negatively influenced as to his moral character and he was prejudiced as a result. In essence, the jury thought that he was dangerous and someone capable of doing bad things because of the way the courtroom staff was treating him.

A third issue I argued was that on the first day of the trial, the defendant had to wear a prison uniform because the prison staff lost his suit. I argued that this further prejudiced the jury's perception of him – they saw him as a criminal rather than a respectably dressed citizen. The State argued that the blue top with a pocket on the front didn't look like a prison uniform, and therefore was unlikely to have caused any prejudice.

In sum, the defense argued that, in light of all the circumstances, the defendant was subjected to a prejudiced jury trial and a miscarriage of justice occurred. I argued the trial court's decision should be reversed and a new trial conducted. The State argued that any errors which occurred were harmless, and that even absent those errors, the facts overwhelmingly proved his guilt. According to the State, the trial court's verdict should be affirmed.

All of the above was our class assignment, wrapped in a forty page, appellate brief. The term "brief" is oxymoronic, as in addition to all our explanations, analyses, and arguments, we also needed to include a full list of all the cases we cited. My argument was built around fifty cases, some Constitutional statutes, and a ton of other sources. Correctly drafting citations for the law you rely upon is a full time job. Some of my classmates used citation-creating software. I did it old school.

Last semester's "open memo" assignment paled in comparison. This brief took an unbelievable amount of time. Hours and hours of research. Hours and hours of writing. Hours and hours of rewrites. The research alone was astounding.

Let me break down the approach for writing such a large paper as this. You start off with your first issue, which was the "shackles" fact, and then you search for cases with facts similar to that. This general search alone yields thousands of cases, so you narrow it by adding "Courtroom" into your query. This drops the results to a few hundred. Narrow that more by including "juror" and "prejudice," and the results continue to dwindle. The goal is to narrow the search enough to yield only a few relevant cases.

The next step is to prioritize the cases based on influence. The more similar the facts, the more influential the case. You also need to identify cases of "Mandatory Authority," meaning lower courts must follow the announced rule. Mandatory Authority is binding on other courts. For example, the trial court is the lowest branch in the Florida court system. Therefore, trial courts must follow case law made in the higher state courts (the appellate court in their district and the Supreme Court of Florida). The appellate court, on the other hand, because it is higher than the trial court, need not follow the lower court's rules, but it must follow law "handed down" by the Supreme Court of Florida. The Supreme Court of Florida is the highest court in the state, but it is bound by the rulings of the United States Supreme Court, the highest court in our nation.

At the end of the day, after you complete your research, you you have a pyramid of courts to work through and "rank." This is a critical part of your presentation, because if you find a case that helps you, it may be trumped by a case from a higher court. So your research does not stop at finding the "right" case, you have to trace it all the way up the pyramid to see if any other court overturned that decision. And if you don't and end up arguing "bad law," you will lose the appeal. Much better to address the good and bad cases together and argue why the good cases should be relied upon and why the bad cases should not.

I wouldn't have thought law school could be so evil, but the paper was due the Monday after Spring Break. So, no vacation for most. As it turned out, just last year, most people didn't finish until a few hours before the deadline; some only minutes before.

Good thing I did not go on vacation. My Mac was about nine years old and about halfway through typing the Brief, my "A" button stopped typing. Oh shit. Every student's worst nightmare: computer trouble right before a deadline. How was I going to finish the next twenty pages with no "A"?

To compound the problem, because mine was such an old model, I couldn't find replacement parts. I was screwed, big time. After wasting six hours on the phone and running around to local stores, I found a dealer in Texas who had a compatible keyboard. Only, it wouldn't arrive until Monday. Since that would obviously not work, I was left to figure out another way.

I decided to finish the paper by replacing all "As" with "Xs." After I finished, I went back through and literally copy and pasted back in all the "As." What at first looked like: "Therefore, we xs the Xppellants in this cxse, feel thxt the Defendxnt wxs denied his fundxmentxl right to x fxir xnd impxrtixl trixl, xnd xs x result, the decision of the lower court should be reversed xnd x new trixl hxd," after untold hours of work it finally became: "Therefore, we as the Appellants in this case, feel that the Defendant was denied his fundamental right to a fair and impartial trial, and as a result, the decision of the lower court should revered and a new trial had." I finished at 2 a.m. with twelve hours to spare.

Fun, fun, fun.

But wait, there's more . . .

Appellate Hell, Part 2

Now that the Brief was done, we set up for Phase Two: Oral Arguments. Yes, we actually got to argue in court; in front of "judges" (granted, the judges were our professors, a few upperclassmen, and a couple of volunteer practicing attorneys).

The Oral Arguments started with the professor dividing up each class into teams of two. Each team argued one side of the same case we prepared for our Appellate Briefs. Luckily, I got paired up with one of my study partners so we already knew how to work well together. We represented the convicted defendant in the appeal. She addressed the first two issues involving voir dire and discrimination. I took the last issue involving the "unnecessary" security measures.

To make things a little more exciting, once they gave us the assignment they simultaneously informed us that we had to be prepared to argue in four days! Four days to prepare our appellate argument??? Needless to say, we started preparing immediately.

When we were done, it turned out that we spent about sixteen to eighteen hours per day, every day, for the four days. I kid you not. We organized everything, we wrote out our introductions and our arguments, we practiced giving them to each other. We critiqued one another, and then we did it all over again. Then over again, and over again. For four days.

Everyone was nervous the morning of oral arguments. I even forgot my belt. Considering I lost nearly twenty pounds since starting school (not working out at all and eating only peanut butter and jelly for four months will have that effect on you), a belt would have helped. So, there I was, minutes before entering court, with my pants sagging.

I danced through the breezeway with one hand on my waist to hold everything together, scanning to see if any of my male classmates were wearing a black belt I could temporarily borrow. No luck.

So, as desperate times all for desperate measures, I ran to the library, grabbed a stapler, stuck it down my pants and carefully, very carefully, stapled my waistline close enough so that my pants didn't fall. Thankfully, with my blazer buttoned, it wasn't noticeable. Problem solved.

Learn from my mistake people, because you don't need this stress before an argument. Make sure you have everything you need before you leave your house in the morning, like a belt … but just in case keep an extra stapler in your car.

The mock-trial courtroom would have been a spectacle to any onlookers in those minutes before session. Some of us pacing up and back in the aisles, others sitting anywhere they could spread out their notes. Everyone nervously rehearsing.

The judges entered the room wearing black robes. Per courtroom etiquette, we all rose as they walked in, single file, and took their seats behind the bench. They spoke among themselves for a few minutes, perhaps small talk about Monday Night

Football? Perhaps about the fate of the universe? Perhaps about the incredibly stupid kid covered in staples? I don't know. Meanwhile, we sweated and waited with mounting fear and anticipation. Finally the room fell silent and the Chief Judge looked over and nodded at us. That was our cue.

My partner took the helm first. We were only allotted fifteen minutes to present our side. That sounds like a lot, but when the judges interrupt to ask questions every ten seconds, it's hard to get in a single word of what you've prepared. You're allowed to have your notes with you, but there's not time to look for points or answers. You have to know your argument cold, including case citations, or you're a goner.

Unfortunately for my study partner, the judges were rough on her. Very rough. In fact, as soon as she started her intro (maybe 45 seconds into it), she was blasted with questions. One after another. She did a good job answering and returning to her own argument, but each time she started to speak again she got blasted again. One judge was particularly confrontational. This judge had a follow-up question for every question, whether her own question or another judge's. She did not stop.

This sort of exchange makes it extremely difficult to stay focused because the judge's questions end up controlling what is actually discussed. Not what you prepared for, necessarily, but what the judge's want to discuss. Under these circumstances, it's easy to get confused and lose track of where you are. It did not take long to understand that was the point of this exercise. I could see my partner losing track, and I started to fear for my turn.

Of the allotted fifteen minutes, the judge's questions took nearly thirteen of that. Then suddenly, one of the judges interrupted her in the middle of an answer to announce that her time was up. My partner nodded, thanked the court, and sat down. She was wide eyed, flushed, and subtly trembling. The tone had been set.

Next up was one of the "State's Attorneys." He was a poor orator, used bad law, and stuttered nervously. I wondered if that was deliberate because, in response, the judges cut him some slack. They didn't ask too many questions, barely interrupted, and even gave him nods of reassurance. He got to spell out his entire argument, give his conclusion, and take his seat before his time expired.

"Wow! That was unfair," I thought to myself as I rose to give my argument.

In light of what I had seen so far, I decided to just go for it. In my most powerful voice, I opened with "May it please this honorable court, my name is Michael Reppas, I represent John Smith… an innocent man wrongfully convicted of a crime for reasons that are unacceptable to our standards of fairness and justice. Reasons that, I hope, you will consider egregious enough to overturn his conviction and allow him his Constitutional right to a fair day in court." Then I just kept going. I actually got through my entire intro before they interrupted with their first question. I answered it partially, informed them that my next point would give a more comprehensive explanation, and asked to proceed. They seemed impressed and nodded in approval. On I went.

From that point on, I was in control. I nailed every question. I was articulate and spoke clearly. I demonstrated utmost respect for the "Honorable Judges." I never interrupted, I always asked permission to continue, and I never directly contradicted their points. Better than telling them they were wrong, I gave arguments in support of my alternative conclusions.

Throughout my fifteen minutes, it seemed to me that the judges were quite attentive; maybe even enjoying my presentation. One judge even asked a non-factual question about my views on peremptory challenges.

"Shouldn't an attorney have the right to take a person off of a jury panel if they don't want them?" I answered: "Yes, but such right is not unlimited. Peremptory challenges may not be used to discriminatorily dismiss a prospective juror because of gender or race. That's discrimination. That's something that must not be tolerated. But where the purpose is nondiscriminatory, the right to excuse unqualified jurors should be protected."

Then all the sudden, my time was up. So I thanked them and took my seat.

My opposing counsel was up next. He did okay; nothing special. I noted all the cases he cited, so I could counter them during my rebuttal. After he finished, I had the opportunity for a one-minute rebuttal.

I went back up, confidently, and explained why his interpretations were flawed, and why his arguments failed. I did a good job, but I exceeded my time limit. Not a huge mistake, but I should have been more mindful. Again, I thanked the judges and took my seat.

A few minutes later the judges asked us to step outside while they went over their notes. Because this was a "mock" trial, they weren't going to make a ruling to decide who prevailed. Instead, they were reviewing their notes in order to give our performance reviews.

We were called back in after ten anxiety-ridden minutes.

The judges admitted they were really hard on my partner. They applauded her for citing the right cases and knowing them thoroughly. They also said she managed to get through a difficult argument without making any big mistakes.

They told the student with the stutter that he did a good job, even though we all knew that wasn't true. They gave him a few pointers on how stay at ease, and said overall he did just fine.

Then it was my turn. They told me I did really well, but needed to raise my voice a little (which I couldn't believe, because I thought I was really loud and booming, but I guess I was wrong). They also gave me a couple of hints for the Moot Court Competition[41] , and told me that if I made a few changes I could go "all the way." Wow!

It turned out that the "Most Stressful and Challenging Hour and a Half of First Year" wasn't that bad… at least not for me. To be honest, I actually enjoyed it. Yahoo! I was progressing in this metamorphosis; now I was "acting" like a lawyer!

---

41 More on this later.

36

I Got a Job ... a Job, a Job, a Job!

Guess who got a summer job? That's right. I did! It wasn't a paying job, of course, but it would be great experience which, I hoped, would make me more appealing and qualified when I did start looking for a real job after I got to Point "B."

Apparently, a judge was looking to hire a summer clerk and someone gave him my name and number after the Appellate Oral Arguments (I don't know who). A few days after, I got a call telling me to come in for an interview with the judge. How lucky was that?

Now because competition for any legal job is fierce, you need to stand out; find a way to be remembered. Resumes all look the same and experienced lawyers and judges meet potential employees constantly. So make sure you have an angle. Find a way to make an impression so that after you leave the interview, you're remembered. This will give you a leg up in securing a job. I hope . . .

I walked into the judge's office, shook his hand, and told him it was an honor to meet him. A good hand shake is a great way to be remembered.

The judge was a bit eccentric. His shelves were filled not with law books, but with coffee mugs from around the world. Most judges, scholars, and lawyers, probably to impress visitors and clients, display their publications, diplomas, and awards; not this guy. Perfect. I had found an angle.

"Drink a lot of coffee?" I casually asked. He laughed and said he was a collector, not a drinker. He had cups from all around the world. I seized the opportunity to develop a personal connection, and asked if he had traveled to those places himself. Good thinking that was. We really dove into it – who gave him what cup, where, when, etc. I did my best to seem genuinely interested, and made sure to laugh at a few of his anecdotes.

Some of the cups were from Europe, places where I had visited before. I asked specific questions about those cups, showing him that I was a "well-traveled" person, and also trying to let him know that I had a good bit of knowledge about world politics. I worked in "totalitarian regime" and "hegemony in the European market" – concepts learned by every Political Science major – to let him know how smart I was (or how smart I was trying to be to impress him!). He seemed to notice and appreciate it as we spoke at length about the European experience.

I gave him my resume and as we continued to speak, he again noticed and was impressed to learn of my experience and knowledge of foreign affairs. I was feeling really good when I told him that I was Greek. To which he immediately jumped into personal anecdotes about his Greek friends and their restaurants. I still don't believe it, but we talked for two and a half hours. Finally, his wife called and he had to go... but not before he offered me the job.

I was going to clerk for a hotshot judge. YES, YES, YES! Good thing I took Appellate Advocacy, because I'd be working at the court of appeals. The work would be very similar to the stuff I was doing for my brief and oral argument assignments. As I understood it, I'd mostly be summarizing appellate briefs for the judge (but real cases this time). I'd have to pick out the "pertinent" cases that each side used, pull and brief them, and outline everything for the judge. The best part of this is that I would get to attend court and observe real oral arguments from skilled appellate attorneys. This was going to be incredible!

The only downside was that it was a no-pay gig, so I'd have to get a job waiting tables to pay the rent, etc. Happy to do so for this opportunity. "Would you like some more iced tea?"

37

Catch Up

We had five weeks left in the semester. You know what that means – time to start prepping for exams. I was on par with most of my classes – cases were read and briefed, and I was in a decent frame of mind to start studying. I maintained my outlines, and had a few supplements. For these classes, it would be mostly review.

But there was always the neglected class. For me, it was Civil Procedure and I knew it was going to be hard to get ready. I hated Civ Pro and Civ Pro hated me. My professor bored the death out of me so I couldn't stand going to class. As a result, I hadn't done anything in class for weeks! This meant I had a semester's worth of Civ Pro to learn in the last five weeks. Could I do it? Probably not, but I had a plan.

There's a famous professor named Arthur Miller, who made a ton of money selling his Civ Pro class on compact discs. I'm investing a huge chunk of time to listen to his course, and I hope it's enough. On top of that, I invested in supplements and several awesome outlines I scammed off a Three-L.

I rolled the dice a bit here (more on that in a bit), because I decided not to use my case book. Stupid? Maybe... probably... but for me this subject was too complicated and precise to be taught by a professor that could not keep my attention for more than two minutes. I hadn't relied on him to teach me anything, hadn't briefed any cases, hadn't even read any cases. I was doing this one on my own.

You might find, once or twice in school, that you have to teach yourself. I couldn't get anything of value out of class, so it was up to me to both teach and to learn, and I did.

The main reason I did this was because first semester I killed myself with this professor, doing everything he ordered, step-by-step, no deviation from his instructions... and came out with a "C." So, I think that the error in my strategy was my method of attack. I briefed every case assigned, I took meticulous notes in each class, and I studied his material as s devout monk would study the Bible.

Not this time.

My prediction: a solid "B."

| VOICE FROM THE FUTURE: | That was a stupid decision.

38

Moot Court Competitions

Moot Court is a law school organization for mock-trial competitors. Pretty much every law school has a moot court team. The set-up of moot court is identical to the Appellate Brief and Oral Argument exercises we went through in class. Students first have to try out for the team, and those who make it participate in mock trials against other school teams. It is a very prestigious extracurricular activity that can really make participants stand out in their class. It's great for the practice and the resume.

The try-out is exactly like the Oral Argument. You pair up with a team mate, get assigned one side or the other and prepare and argue the case at trial in front of judges. The best team wins, so it's important to choose your partner carefully. [42]

Because my study partner wanted nothing to do with more court competitions, I chose a friend from another section. He

---

[42] Though there is also the runner-up way of making the team. Some people, even if they don't win at trial, are offered to submit their Briefs for evaluation. If your writing is outta this world, you might make the team after all.

was a smart guy so I was sure we'd do well, even though we both argued for the defense and argued the same issue in our Appellate Oral Arguments. That gave us a slight disadvantage. I think the better teams are the diversified teams, in which each partner has opposite experience. It makes for a more comprehensive team.

I volunteered to take the unfamiliar issue. I felt I could handle it, and therefore, we'd stand a better chance of winning. Besides, he'd proven to me, in more ways than one, that he was a true and loyal friend, and since he had more exam-prep stress than I, I was happy to help him out by taking on the extra load.

Anyway, it wasn't as if I was starting from scratch. I had already exhaustively researched both sides of the issue, had done a forty-five-page paper on it, and my oral argument partner gave me her notes from our class arguments. So basically all I had to do was write an intro, memorize the pertinent cases, and practice, practice, practice. It was a lot of work, but not as bad as I originally thought. I felt ready for Round One.

Unlike before, in this try-out a decision was actually rendered at the end of the proceeding.

This was intensity at its best; a real competition!

--------- Moot Court Competitions, Round One ----------

I was the first to the stand, and the firing squad opened fire within thirty seconds. I deflected, I dodged, and I repelled the attacks as best I could. After countless questions, I got the opportunity to get to my own arguments. Thirty seconds into that and the barrage began anew. On this went throughout my entire time.

Moot Court Competitions

And the questions were damn hard. Fair, but hard. I was prepared and I got through it. I think my answers may not have been considered "high art," but they were competent.

This time, however, I wasn't without error. I got a little caught up with the facts of one of the cases I cited. In my head, I had jumbled the background facts and procedural posture, the reasoning behind the decision, and the standard of review. I definitely lost points for that.

Soon enough, the court assistant raised the five-minute time card. I needed to focus fast to get through my argument and close. I managed to muddle successfully through the rest of the case, made my closing points, and thanked the judges with no time to spare.

My partner was next and absolutely killed. He did unbelievably well; definitely better than I did. He was familiar with the issue, and was ready. Here I was, thinking I was going to pull the team, but he blew me away. We both did well, but he exceeded and excelled.

Time for opposing counsel. And who approached the podium with a snarl on her lips? The Lizard! She went up, cocky, and started by directly telling the court what their decision should be. She got to speak uninterrupted for about a minute before the judges started nailing her with questions. It was great. They reamed her. She tried to get out, but couldn't do it.

They maintained the assault by asking her to address arguments we had made. She tried countering our arguments, but was unsuccessful. The judges repeatedly chided her by saying, "We don't buy it. What's your next argument, counselor?"

My partner and I sat the edge of our seats. We knew a final

blow was coming, and we couldn't wait to see it hit her. And then it came and she was cornered by the Socratic Method. She fell defeated, and gave up. The judges had sufficiently confused and overwhelmed her, and when the Chief Judge asked her if it was at all possible that the jury had, in fact, been influenced by the security measures taken at trial, the shackles, she had nothing left to say but, "I suppose perhaps they might have been influenced."

And just like that, the Lizard conceded. She actually conceded! And just like that, we won Round One, and they were out. Though arguments played out to the end, the case was over.

When her co-counsel approached the stand with all the world on her shoulders, she couldn't hold it. She shook, quivered, and stumbled her way through. She was obviously nervous, and could muster only a mediocre effect. It was over, but we still weren't done. Our side still had time for rebuttal.

It was my chance for the slam dunk. I approached the stand, thanked the judges again for their time, and simply stated "Your Honors, opposing counsel conceded that the jury was influenced by the security measures taken at trial. As a result, the Defendant did not receive a fair and impartial trial, and for this reason we ask that you reverse the decision of the trial court and remand this case so that the Defendant may have his Constitutional Right to a fair trial. Thank you." Then I took my seat.

We waited in the hallway while the judges deliberated. My partner and I visibly confident; the girls visibly defeated. We were called back in, individually critiqued, and then informed of the judges' decision. WE WON! Yes, the sweet taste of victory!

But it wasn't over. In two days we were to battle again in Round Two.

Moot Court Competitions

---------- Moot Court Competitions, Round Two ---------

Our opponents in Round Two were two "golden" students. The first, Tracey, was the prodigy child of two attorneys. Apparently, her parents grilled her night and day for a week to prepare. The second, Cassandra, was a friend from my section who made Dean's List and nailed her Appellate Oral Argument.

The competition was hot. Neither my partner nor I come from legal families or made Dean's List. Still, we were confident, and determined to prove ourselves.

Again, I was up first. I began with a steady confidence in my voice, and got through twenty seconds before the questioning unleashed. I was taken; from one point to the next, from one case to another, from one side of the argument to the opposing side, but this time I was ready.

I answered every question with a quiet enthusiasm. I "educated" the judges regarding the law at issue and how the lower court had erred. I was asked questions simultaneously by different judges. I assumed it was a test of my focus, and remembered to address and answer each in turn. I was on it. I even articulately answered questions regarding my partner's arguments. They kept going, and so did I. I got through it without conceding any significant or harmful points, and (I think) successfully returned their attentions back to my points. I was sharp. I felt like I did extremely well.

My Partner faced the same attack. Unfortunately, he didn't do as well as before. He wasn't able to work his argument into his answers. He was completely on the defensive; answering their questions and just waiting for more. Not good.

Next, the superstars took the helm. The first did a solid job. She screwed up a couple of facts, but nothing irredeemable. The second lady followed in the same fashion. They both carried their voices well, and did admirable jobs. Still, I sensed we were ahead.

All I had to do was nail my rebuttal. Though it wasn't as easy a task as my Round One rebuttal, I did a good job. I gave counter examples to their arguments, provided justification for my interpretations, and smoothly closed by reiterating that a correct legal interpretation supports our position.

Despite the overall "kill or be killed" mentality, we were all cordial as we waited together in the hallway during the judges' deliberation. We matter of factly gave each other positive, constructive criticism, admired each other's strengths, and shook hands. We were genuinely impressed by each other, and confident enough to give well-deserved accolades. It was a real departure from the usual law school/moot court competition animosity.

But the news was a bummer. We lost.

VOICE FROM THE FUTURE: There are many opportunities to stand out in law school. I didn't make the Moot Court, but apparently, I did well enough to be invited to join the International Moot Court team. What is that, like the JV team? Interestingly enough, I ended up spending the majority of the rest of law school, my post-grad LL.M. (in International Law), and the first 15 years of my career, practicing international law. Just goes to show that, maybe, everything does happen for a reason. Take chances in law school – there are so many opportunities, and you never know which one will impact your professional career and define your success. I thought I lost by not making the Moot Court team, but

I actually won by making the International Moot Court team.

International Law Society

One morning the current and incumbent International Law Society presidents approached me. They had become aware of my focus in international law, and asked me to join their organization, the "ILS." They told me that the Secretary Chair was coming open for the following year, and they wanted to groom me for the position.

My interest and commitment to international law had been on the rise. Getting a spot on the International Law Moot Court team and now joining the Board of the ILS was a great combo. I immediately thanked them and accepted the offer.

WOW! This was the first time I had an official title that sounded impressive. "Head Bussboy," not so impressive, but "Mr. Secretary?" Totally cool, I could get used to it. Hopefully by third year I'd be able rise to the rank of "President."

A note in my metamorphosis here: I was starting to take this stuff seriously. I was beginning to build a sophisticated resume, and started to feel like a real lawyer. I felt confident and could only wonder, what's next?

39

Crunch Time

One week until exams. Regular classes have ended and now it's really crunch time. The outline scamming game is going wild and people are freaking out once again. My original five weeks of crunch time have whittled down and there are only three days left.

But I'm not nervous. I can do this! To boost my confidence, I remember what Harold Ramis said in 'Stripes' when all the cadets were doubting whether they could learn the maneuvers they needed to graduate the next day. "We can do this . . . we have four hours . . . I learned two semesters of Biology in four hours. We can do this."

Let's see if that hold true for Civ Pro.

40

Law Review Write-On Competition

As if moot court try-outs weren't enough, I decided to try out for Law Review, the most prestigious law school organization of them all. Hands down. It is the law school creme de la creme, and every big firm wants to see "Law Review" on prospective associates' resumes. In fact, most big firms won't even consider a candidate who was not on Law Review. 'Nuf said. It's VIP people. VIP.

Every school has its own Law Review which annually publishes journals containing judge's, professor's and some student legal papers. At our school, like many schools in the country, students in the top five percent of their class get a "walk-on." They didn't have to submit any writing for review before getting an invitation to join; they automatically made the team because of their grades. The rest of us had to enter the write-on competition and hope for the best.

The competition started the day after the last day exams. The professors heading up the Law Review informed all applicants not to make any summer plans until ten days after the last day of exams. Ten days. That's how long it takes to complete the two-part try-out. First, you had to research and draft a fifteen-page essay. The second part was a Blue Book exam. The scores from these two components, plus your GPA, were factored together to give an overall score. There were (up to) four available spots this year for write-on applicants (those moving into their second and third year) – and the top scores got in. As with everything else in Law School, there was incredible competition and the pressure was through the roof.

The write-on is basically an essay test to see how well you write in a limited amount of time. They give you one week to research and write an academic essay on their topic. It is an issue that you have to analyze and argue as would a legal scholar. Our subject was to decide whether the Florida Bar's rules prohibiting attorney solicitation in certain situations was Constitutional. It was not a hypothetical case - it was a real one that went through all the courts in the State of Florida (including the Supreme Court of Florida), and was, at the time of our writing the essay, before the Supreme Court of the United States on a Writ of Certiorari. What we had to do was not only analyze and argue the issue, but also predict how the U.S. Supreme Court would rule.

It was a lot of work. I mean a LOT of work. Fortunately, the Judge gave me the week off to do it – he made Law Review when he went to law school. The restaurant where I was working nights also gave me the week off, even though none of them knew what the hell Law Review was; I guess it just sounded impressive.

I worked and worked and worked and worked. I did my best and turned it in on time. Of course, my old computer died on me right in the middle of the project (in accordance with the principles of Murphy's Law), so I used one of my buddy's to finish up. I think it went pretty well.

END RESULT: I did not make the team as a write-on.

VOICE FROM THE FUTURE: Don't cry for me Argentina. Keep reading, because I did end up on the Law Review and you need to know how I accomplished that.

41

Interning With The Judge

My summer judicial clerkship was awesome! The work was interesting and challenging. The people were cool. The experience was educational. And I got a fantastic addition to my resume.

The State Court of Appeals hears non-federal cases that have already gone through trial in the Circuit Court. The basic procedure after a party decides to file an appeal is to prepare their Appellant Brief – which is exactly what I did the prior semester in Appellate Advocacy. Once the "appealing party" (a/k/a "Appellant") has filed his/her brief, the opposing side (a/k/a "Appellee") must draft and file an Answer Brief.

Once both briefs and all necessary supplemental documents have been filed, the appeal is assigned to a judge for review.[43] Once a judge gets a new case assigned, his research assistant (a/k/a

---

43 There is a random "spin-the-wheel" rotation system for assigning new cases to the judges, by the way.

"RA") gets to work first. RAs are invariably law school graduates who were on Law Review, did fantastically well academically, and got the job over literally hundreds of other applicants.

It is the job of the RA to prepare a synopsis of the facts of the case and summarize what happened in the trial court. Note that these are the "facts" the trial court determined to be the actual "facts" of the dispute, not what each side claimed were the facts. Big difference there.

After the RA finishes the synopsis, it is passed to summer interns, like me, to do the grunt work. Our job was to read the briefs thoroughly and make a list of all the pertinent cases the parties cited in their briefs. From that list we pulled each case and briefed each one without bias to either side. The judge relied on our briefs to determine, uninfluenced by adversarial lawyers, the proper Rule of Law on the issue.

Most of my time was spent pulling and briefing cases, but the reward was being able to attend the actual oral arguments, where we were allowed to sit in a special, "We Are Interns," section and watch the show. The judge, alongside two other judges, would "preside" over the hearing when both sides made their appellate arguments.

So I got to sit there in court and listen to real attorneys argue cases I had thoroughly researched. I got to study and learn from their styles and techniques, and yes, it is very similar to Law & Order, except that they speak in legal terms that only attorneys can understand and also, no one dared pound on the podium or yell "I object" to the judges. Interestingly enough, Mariska Hargitay was there, so that was cool, but the best part of the experience was being able to hear what the judges liked and disliked about each attorney's presentation in their chambers after it was all over. That was indeed the best part.

I was also allowed to attend court, even for the cases which I hadn't briefed. I did this every chance I got. I just couldn't get enough of the action – watching the attorneys, learning what worked, mentally recording what didn't. Some of the attorneys were great; others were pathetic. Really. Sometimes the judges would agree with their arguments, other times they'd interrupt an attorney with their questions. Once I saw a judge tell an attorney half way through his argument to take his seat because he had heard enough. Ouch! It was really cool, for me anyway, not the embarrassed attorney, obviously.

Judicial clerkships are rare to come by, because there are so many applicants and so few spots. At the Appellate Courthouse where I was working, only four RAs were from Florida law schools, the rest were N.Y.U., Stanford, Harvard, and Yale.

VOICE FROM THE FUTURE: I strongly recommend that you observe as many trials and oral argument as you can. It's not TV, it's real. If you are thinking about going to law school you should experience a real trial before jumping in. And no, you don't have to be in law school to go watch. Most court sessions are open to the public. Just go to the nearest courthouse, ask security at the entrance and they should be able to help. Sit there for as long as you like. One helpful hint here: dress appropriately, be polite to the clerks, bailiffs, and the courtroom staff, be quiet, and enjoy the show.

42

Transferring To A Different School

Remember KJ? The "Jerky Boy" that everyone accused of holding out on them during the group study exam period? Well, he got his wish: he transferred to a school near his hometown. His family was there, his friends were there, and now his future was there. Going to school in Florida was hard for him; he missed his family and friends, and always wished that he had been accepted to a school closer to home. He did well enough at our school to transfer to his first choice – the Law School that did not accept him last year. Apparently a few Two-L spots opened up at the end of the year (either from drop-outs, transfers, or from students who flunked out), so this time his "re-application," which included his transcript from our Law School, was enough to get him in. He left so fast it wasn't until after he was gone that the rest of us found out what happened. A little rude on his part by not saying goodbye to anyone, but in retrospect I suppose, a fitting exit for that character.

VOICE FROM THE FUTURE: A lot of students who don't get accepted to their top choice school take this same approach. So, if you don't get into the school of your dreams when first applying, don't be discouraged. Choose one of your back up schools (especially one which is affordable), and focus on one task only: get good grades. If you're successful, you'll have the opportunity to transfer to a higher-tiered school. The higher your class ranking the better. Maintain communication with your dream school's Office of Admissions, make sure to meet all their requirements, and stay focused. It can work out if you are patient, diligent, and a bit lucky.

43

In. Cheat. Out.

Once we received our second semester grades, we got to find out which students were asked not to return; a very nice way of saying who flunked out. This vignette details the exploits of a few students who were "released" at the end of their first year.

Seven students were put on academic probation after the first semester. Some of them were cool, others were not. But law school is not about being "cool;" it's about being a good student. Even if you are not the most academically gifted person in the world you can get through law school, if you are dedicated and bust your hump during the school year. If you goof around too much or put a half-ass effort into studying, the only way you're going to get by is if you are very intelligent. But if you're not a genius, you'd better study your ass off. Some didn't figure that out until it was too late.

Before being kicked out, students were put on academic probation when their grades fell under a 2.0. Their second semester was a probationary term, and if they didn't raise their cumulative grade point to over a 2.0 they would be asked to leave. That meant that getting a 2.0 in their second semester wasn't going to cut it – they had to get high enough grades so that the average of their first and second semester grades was over a 2.0.

One of the friends I played music with was put on academic probation after the first semester. His GPA was a 1.9. Maybe this guy didn't bust his hump the first semester, but he definitely did his second. He failed Legal Writing, and as a consequence, he had to do make-up work for that class during the second semester, while simultaneously keeping up with all his other classes. I never saw him. He was always in the library studying. He gave it his best effort, but in the end his grades for the second semester were a flat 2.0 and he was asked to leave.

He did not go quietly into that good night, however, and instead, petitioned the school to stay. He wrote a long paper – actually a third year friend of ours wrote it for him – and told the school that the only reason his grades weren't better was because he had to do the make-up work for Legal Writing. Of course, there was a lot more to it, but that was the main gist of it. Believe it, or not, it worked. He was allowed to stay, but once again he was on probation – he was given one last chance to bring his cumulative over a 2.0.

Some other kids who were "dismissed" were not as lucky. One girl who was on probation ended up failing Contracts II. She also filed a petition to stay in school, but her petition was denied so she was packing up to go back home to the same job she had before law school (but now with an additional $75,000 debt, not to mention having to live with the stigma of having failed out of law school). I was really sorry for her, but that was the unfortunate reality of law school. They don't give everybody who gets in a diploma. You have to earn it. I guess I supported that hard-line policy, but it sure did make it hard for those few unfortunates who didn't make the cut. More than a few: fifteen students were expelled out of our class.

I also want to share the story of one particular fellow who was expelled. We nicknamed him "Guido" because of the mafia-wanna-be way he spoke and carried himself. He was Cuban-American, who thought he was Italian. Regardless, let me tell you, this guy lived a dream life his first year. Flaunting wealth and making sure that everyone knew it. He drove a Porsche the first semester, then traded it in for an NSX the second semester. We're talking about the kind of guy who has no other goal in life but to project a facade of how perfect he is.

Guido set the stage immediately upon arriving at school. He moved into the dorms with the rest of us, and that first night he ended up sleeping with another first year student . . . the Lizard. The next day he went around telling everyone about his conquest and working in the fact that he had a Master's Degree, although he wouldn't tell anyone what he actually got the Master's Degree in. "Perhaps they offer a Master's in Bullshit," one of my friends offered when we discussed it. Probably. Anyway, suffice it to say that most people hated him and the others simply loathed him.

Although we did not know it at the time, Guido was on probation after the first semester. In retrospect, this would not have been a shock to any of us had we known at the time. Here's the straw that broke the proverbial camel's back and caused his downfall.

When we were all writing our Open Memos in the first semester, Guido asked one of my buddies to proof his paper and my buddy told us all that it was the most unintelligible thing he had ever read. But my buddy told Guido it was fine because he didn't like him and wanted him to submit a horrible paper to get a horrible grade. So Guido apparently turned in that piece of crap memo and got an "A." How did he do that? Well, it spread through the grapevine that he had an attorney friend of his write it for him (not the same version he gave my friend to read, obviously). That sure would explain the variance in quality from the first draft. The truth finally came out when he had to sit for the end of semester exams and write his essays himself without any hired guns to do it for him.

This "personal accountability" proved to everyone that he was a cheat, and from that point on everyone despised him (even Liz).

When then the second semester arrived, Guido detached himself from everyone, and none of us had much contact with him. In a well planned move, when the second semester exams came around, Guido pulled the "note from the doctor" routine and got his exams pushed back two weeks. During this time he allegedly tried to pay a few students (in unmarked $50 bills) to tell him exactly what was on the exams. As would be expected by competitive driven prospective lawyers, instead of helping him, they turned him in. In the end, it was no shock to anyone that Guido was asked to leave, and his expulsion was greeted with joy by those who knew him.

In. Cheat. Out.

44

Summary Of The First Year

Now that I am officially through my first year of law school, I think it is appropriate to give you a little summary regarding how far this wannabe slacker has come in his personal metamorphosis. Am I a professional yet? The honest answer is "no" because I still couldn't put the title "Esquire" after my name. I'd be a professional when I get to add that "Esq." after my name, not before. Regardless, I definitely developed a more professional attitude and, without question, became a better student.

In short, I learned what it takes to become a professional. I understood the commitment, sacrifice, and sheer determination required. I was committed and willing to sacrifice. I knew the value of the prize, and I knew that I would reach my goal.

I really gave it my best over that first year, and it paid off. Maybe I slacked off a bit the second semester, but I learned my lesson and I was anxious to get back and finish. I wanted to succeed. Even after just one year of law school, I learned the ethics that a true professional must live by to succeed. I knew that once I got that degree I would have to work my butt off to make it and I would do it. I knew that it would not be easy, but nothing worth doing ever is, at least nothing that is worth anything. The journey from "A" to "B" was just shortened by one-third. One year down, two to go.

THE SECOND YEAR

45

Third Semester Classes

Well, here we are again. I was pumped, a Two-L finally! But first thing's first. Let me tell you about my classes. I had Professional Responsibility (called "Pro Rep" or "PR" by the cool kids), Constitutional Law (called "Con Law" by everyone, cool or not), Evidence, Property II (I can't wait), and International Law.

Pro Rep was basically an ethics course telling you how important it is for you to be an honest attorney and laying out all the various forms of punishment that await you if you aren't. Con Law was all about the Constitution, and (according to upper classmen) was the most important law school course you would overtake. Evidence, as the course name suggests, was all about what can and cannot be admitted into evidence at a trial. International Law was about how disputes between people from different countries were handled. Finally, Prop II was a continuation of the same property course I took last semester.

I had classes five days a week, which sadly meant no more three-day weekends. That meant, in turn, that my slacking time would be cut tremendously. I mean, the last thing I needed was free time to actually enjoy myself. No, I wanted to be busy from the time my alarm shrieks me out of bed at dawn until I pass out over my desk at three a.m. That's what I want. None of this "I had a great weekend" crap, no Sir, not for me. I want to get back to the frame of mind where I don't know what is going on in the world (because I won't have time to watch TV) and I won't care. I want to be back to the point where I don't even know there is a world outside of law school. Oh yes, I want to be completely consumed by my studies. Consumed, do you hear me? And I will be.

Last semester I sort-of rebelled against the monastic life I was forced to lead in the first semester and indulged myself by relaxing a bit and only devoting about 85% of my "everything" to Law School. As a result, there was a slight drop in my grades. Not this time!

NO EXCUSES. NOBODY CARES. GET TO WORK!

46

Why The Bootcamp Style of Teaching is Followed in the First Year of Law School

The first year of Law School is deliberately designed to put you through hell.

My Pro Rep professor was one feared man. A real get-in-your-face instructor who lived for the kill. The kind who would stand you up in class and make you recite the Federal Rules, all 85 of them, just for fun. The kind who loved to make first year as difficult as possible. A true Superior Professor.

Once, he had the entire class write down the things we didn't like about first year. He collected our responses and wrote them up on the board. The board was covered with things like: "the cutthroat attitude of students," "the Socratic Method of Teaching" (which is exactly the style that this Superior Professor employed), "the massive work load," "the sense of no-reward for working so hard and getting average grades," and "the lack of care and concern by faculty in regards to the problems faced by students." A lot of serious complaints.

After he shared thirty or so complaints, he responded with the reasons for the first year "Boot Camp."

"Our intention is to beat the values you come here with out of you. Whatever values you brought in, we sought to remove. We do this so that you become dehumanized. We want you to be able to put emotion aside and rationally analyze issues put before you. We want you to be prepared to handle life as an attorney. It is our intent, our purpose, to make the first year as unpleasant as possible; as difficult as possible. If you can't get by the first year, then we don't want you to practice law. We desensitize you so that it doesn't matter who you hate: students, professors, judges, fellow attorneys, or what obstacles get in your way. The first-year experience trains you to be able to handle any legal and work situation. If you can focus throughout first year despite the opposition and obstacles, then you'll be ready for judges, adversarial attorneys, clients, or whomever. You will persevere. We train you to be focused on the end-result.

"Now that you've gotten through the 'Boot Camp,' your legal initiation, we consider you peers. You are no longer unproven trainees. You are combat veterans. In the next two years, you'll be pleased to find that professors will treat you with respect. Rarely will you feel as if a professor intends to embarrass you in front of your peers. You've made it through your initiation and can finally feel like a human being again."

It was Nietzsche's theory at play: "That which does not kill you makes you stronger." Not really a shocking bit of information, but at least it was confirmation that what we felt was legitimate and real. Those bastards were actually and intentionally treating us like crap. I guess his words were meant as a "congratulations," of a sort, and a "welcome to the club" gesture.

VOICE FROM THE FUTURE: If ever, during your first year, you lose sight of why you're in law school, if you start to question your intelligence and capabilities, if a professor gives you a particularly rough ride, come back to this book and read this vignette again.

47

International Law

International Law is basically a "legal" Political Science class that deals with the laws of the international community. If you took Political Science or any other International Relations sort of class as an undergrad, you have the general idea. The main difference is that this class is more intense, more difficult, and packed with more reading and briefing assignments than any undergrad or law school class you'll take.[44] I'm serious. A ton of reading and briefing! A lot, lot, lot of work here!

Thankfully I enjoyed the class and liked what I was studying. I had a strong background in political science and philosophies of law so this class actually interested me. I really enjoyed learning about international relations from a legal perspective and human rights.[45]

---

44 With the exception, of course, of Civil Procedure.

45 VOICE FROM THE FUTURE: I liked this class so much so that I ended up pursuing an LL.M. degree in International Law after graduation. I certainly found my passion.

There are two, main international courts that oversee international relations and disputes and monitor how governments treat their citizens. The International Court of Justice is the court of United Nations, and sits in the "Peace Palace" in The Hague (that's in the Netherlands, near Belgium). Any member of the United Nations, which includes most countries in the world, that has a grievance against another country (for anything from who owns what water or mineral rights, to breaches of contract), can take their dispute to the ICJ. The fundamental purpose of the court is to resolve disputes through an impartial judicial system to avoid war. It's a great concept and institution, and it's reassuring to see this sort of international dispute resolution center at play. The Court may not be perfect, but it's a step in the right direction and away from the "might = right" model.

The International Criminal Court is the court of human rights and humanitarian law. The basic legal principle upon which it stands is that all people have basic human rights which no government can take from them. Rights like the right to live, to eat and breathe, freedom of religion, and the right not to be killed. Stuff that we take for granted here in the U.S. Humanitarian Law essentially deals with "laws of war" a/k/a "laws of engagement." The Court was established after World War II in an effort to punish and "put an end to impunity for" perpetrators of "grave crimes [which] threaten the peace, security, and well-being of the world."

In addition to the class being substantively fascinating for me, I was also excited with and inspired by the professor. He was a really cool guy with a strong, animated, German accent. This professor was so good at his job and had so much crystal clear knowledge of this subject that he never read anything in class. Never. He skipped the nonsense and got straight to the point by explaining precisely what the cases were each actually about. He was clear in his explanations, and even made his lectures engaging. He nailed every question asked by students, even the worthless, irrelevant questions, and then brought us right back to the point of the lesson.

He walked around the room calling on people at random, and asking them to share their thoughts on the cases he assigned. He always followed up their answer with another question to them. However, unlike the first-year Superior Professors, he guided students' thinking to the right issues and points. He didn't harass, belittle or intimidate anyone – he just taught.

I tell you what, the man was brilliant. No matter what stupid answer a student gave him, he got them (and the rest of the class in turn) right back where he wanted us to go or back to the concept he wanted us to understand. As a consequence, we actually covered a tremendous amount of material every class. Necessarily, this meant that we went through a tremendous amount of preparation before every class which entailed anywhere from 50 to 100 pages of reading and briefing (double the normal class).

Another difference between this class and every first-year class was that we had the option to write a term paper which could count up to 75% of our final grade. The paper was supposed to be about a legal subject in the international field, and we could pick any topic related to the course.

The only problem in writing a paper like this, with a 35-page minimum, was that it would take a lot of time. A lot of time. Plus, there was still a final exam. So not only did you have to bust your hump for every class, and every other class, but you also had to find the time to write a solid paper and still study for a final. For me it was a no-brainer. I would write the paper because then I wouldn't have to rely solely on the exam for my final grade.

My topic revolved around the issue of when countries used sanctions and military power to affect the outcome of a civil war, like the one in Yugoslavia. What I wanted to find out in researching and writing this paper was, by what legal right could the United States and/or the United Nations, as examples, enter a foreign country and force them to stop fighting against each other. Morally the answer was simple: we don't want them to kill each other, but legally the answer was a lot more complicated. It is *their* country after all. Shouldn't they be allowed to do whatever they want in it, even kill each other? There is a political concept called "territorial sovereignty," which means that every country is a master of its own domain – within its borders, every country is their own ruler – nobody can order a country to do something, unless, of course, they go to war with them and subsequently take them over and force them to do what they want. But outside of that scenario, no country is allowed to invade the space of another country without that country's permission. That is an act of war, right?

I wanted to analyze the legal rights that justify one country entering another country without that government's permission. That's an invasion, right? I wanted to delve into the human right laws that say "yes" you can go in there and stop a genocide. "Yes," you can go in there and stop widespread torture of the innocent. But I was troubled by how this "moral right" threatened the concept of territorial sovereignty. I wanted to delve into that debate and find out exactly why. I hoped that when I was done I would be able to predict how successful a "good intentioned invasion" would be in the future and whether humanitarian intervention could be distinguished from simple regime change policy. Was it legit or just a political move to spread one country's influence and control? That's why I was devoting so much time to this – I was driven to know why.

48

Get Off Your Soapbox ...
Or I'll Push You Off

Our International Law professor left for about three weeks for a seminar, and, as a result, we had guest lecturers on various international law related topics. During one of these lectures, one of my classmates who believed herself to be a deep political thinker, raised her hand and began speaking in the middle of class, when the guest professor was discussing one particular case involving a dispute over cargo damaged in international waters. It wasn't even a question; more like a political commentary on capitalism, democracy, and starving children.

As soon as she started talking, the whole class started mumbling. People were saying, "Oh my God, here she goes." It was just wasting class time. Nobody wanted to hear her thoughts, she wasn't the professor. The guest professor apparently agreed and after listening to her for about two straight minutes, he interrupted her and started to correct her on what she was saying.

She fought back, telling him that what she was saying had to be right because that's the way the world worked. Then he went off. He said she was "unschooled in the fundamentals of capitalism" and proceeded to completely rip apart everything that she said. She kept trying to get a word in, but he didn't let her. Piece by piece, he addressed the "talking points" she went on about and he succinctly and passionately explained how "simple opinions" were not for legal scholars, and that a "heightened awareness" and "educated opinions" were what was required by international lawyers.

It was great. Everybody really enjoyed class that day because she finally got what she had coming.

People, learn from that experience. Don't be that student. People see through it, people are annoyed by it, people look down on it. Save your political opinions for your family and friends. Keep it on topic. This is Law School, get off your Soapbox!

49

A Different Professor Makes
All the Difference

You will recall that I hated my Property class last year, so I decided to take the Prop II class with a different professor, hoping that this decision might have a positive effect on my negative disposition.

Turns out it was a great decision. The class was so enjoyable that I actually wanted to brief the cases and actually go to class. We studied landowner/tenant rights, buying houses, and property sales. The professor gave really nice hypotheticals, and discussed what we should do as attorneys in tough situations.

She taught us all the practical stuff. How to check deeds, and make sure buyers were getting the right title. "Title" is basically an instrument which tells you that a seller actually owns the house he/she is selling without any liens (meaning, they own it free and clear). She also taught us about brokers (the people who actually do the marketing and selling for companies like Century 21, etc.), their fees, why they get them, why they should get them, why they don't get them, and on and on. It was interesting to learn the real details around buying and selling property. A different professor makes all the difference.

50

Constitutional Law:
Great Class. Bad Prof.

Con Law is "the most important class you'll take in law school." Unfortunately for me, it was also the most boring class I took in law school. The subject was important and the cases were interesting, but the professor was dreadful!

The course was, unsurprisingly, about the constitution: the rights we have under the constitution, the cases which have been instrumental in establishing and developing our rights as citizens, and the entire foundation upon which our country was built. It should have been exciting, but Mr. Monotone was... just... soooooo... slooooow... and... monotonous... .

He covered one case per class. That's it. The other Con Law professor got through at least three or four cases per class. Our professor beat the hell out of each case; going into every tiny detail. It would have been better if he had only focused on the black letter law; the reasoning and ruling. For this guy though, it was not just the outcome which is important, he thinks it's important to know why each judge decided the way they did based on their legal opinions as well as their personal beliefs. These details, according to Captain Exciting, delve into society's true nature; it's problems and effects on our rights as US citizens.

He's right, of course, but it is extremely difficult to stay focused in his class. He just moves too slow to keep me engaged. I often leave class with the most wonderful, detailed, constitutional law inspired doodlings you ever have seen. I hope I'm able to learn all this on my own before the final exam, otherwise, I might end up out of law school and forced to live as a starving artist.

51

I Officially Become
A Legal Research Assistant

It is a publish or perish world for professors. You want tenure? Then you need a nice list of publications to justify it. As a result, most professors look for second and third year students to be their research assistants. This basically means that you do their grunt work: look up cases and relevant secondary sources, summarize the law, outline pending cases, whatever they need. There are two perks: (1) it's paid (like $10/hr, but still!), and (2) it looks fantastic on a resume.

There was a new professor at our school, and word got out that he was looking for a research assistant to help with his Philosophy dissertation. Now that was a job with my name written all over it, because I've been well versed in philosophy, particularly Greek philosophy. As a child of proud, Greek immigrant parents, my childhood bookshelves were lined with Socrates, Plato, and Homer (there were a lot of Dr. Seuss books there too, I'll have you know).

I saw an opportunity, and so I went for it. I approached the professor and introduced myself. I let him know that I heard that he was looking for an RA and told him that I wanted to hear more about his topic to see if I could assist him. I told him I was Greek, fluent in Greek, and knowledgeable about philosophy, etc. He told me he was specifically examining one of Plato's last books, ("Laws") and that he wanted a research assistant who would be able to help him study it. I gave him my resume and confidently told him that I was familiar with the book and could help.

A couple days later he gave me a call and said he wanted to see me. I went to his office, and right then and there he offered me the job. I accepted without hesitation! The only thing was that the position required ten hours a week on top of an already packed schedule. So, on top of a regular full-time class schedule, I had my international law paper, International Moot Court, and now 10 hours to study Plato. Sleep be damned!

52

Of Course You Can Have Sex With A Client

So one day, I'm sitting in Pro Rep and the prof is going on about what lawyers can and can't ethically do, as usual. I'm sort of nodding off, but I hear him say the words loyalty, trust, confidence (all of which is collectively known as a "fiduciary duty"). So anyway this prof loves giving hypotheticals. That's how he teaches. It's always, "What if a client comes in to your office and ____ happens? Which rule of Professional Conduct applies to that situation?"

So on this particular day, the class is almost done and the prof suddenly asks no one in particular if you can have sex with a client.

What? Did I hear that right? I decided to look up at the prof to confirm. Anyone with half a brain knows that when you look directly into the eyes of a professor he will call on you. Anyway, before I realized what I had done, he called out to me: "Reppas! Can you have sex with a client?"

The room suddenly went silent and all eyes shifted to me.

I wasn't really sure how to answer since I hadn't read any of the ethical rules on that subject yet, so I just said the first thing that came to my mind, which was, "Yes… as long as there are no billable hours involved."

The class liked the joke, and I think the prof did too, but I'm pretty sure that he knew that I didn't have the rule number that he wanted for the answer. He replied, "Ha, ha, very funny, Mr. Reppas. Where in the Rules does it say that?" Two minutes left in class and I'm in the hot seat. I can BS for two minutes, right? I figure that since the course is about "ethics" all I have to do is answer as if I were Dudley Do-Right (the most honest man on the planet—or was that before your time?). I asked myself, Would Dudley Do-Right sleep with his client?

So I answered the prof by saying, "Actually, professor, the Rules say that you cannot have sex with a client." I began to hear angelic music fill my ears. Books and notebooks began to close around me. I felt protected, warm, and calm. But the prof was relentless. "What specific Rule are you referring to, Reppas?" Which was followed by a short, silent pause before everyone's books started slamming shut signaling the end of class. All my friends slammed their books extra hard so the prof would have no doubt that inquisition time was over. And believe it or not, he did. First year hazing was over. The prof wasn't going to get in my face and insult me. He wasn't going to embarrass me in front of the class for not memorizing all the Rules yet. He was cool. He ended class by saying, "Okay everybody, we'll pick up from there." What a great guy.

Wrong! Why? Because I'm walking up the stairs to see another prof, and the Pro Rep prof coincidentally is also walking up the stairs. As he sees me he says, "Reppas, Reppas…well, where does it say that? Can you have sex with a client? Should you be able to do that? Do that research for next class, Reppas. Look that up. I want you to be able to tell me exactly if you can or can't. I want to know what rules apply to that scenario. It's important, Reppas, you need to know that." He nailed me with all this in about fifteen seconds. I nodded in agreement and told him that I would have all the info he wants for the next class.

Since I knew he was going to call on me for the next class, I decided that I had to be prepared. As luck would have it, I was talking with a friend of mine who had already graduated (though not yet passed the Bar) and he told me that he wrote his Senior Writing Requirement on that same subject. Perfect. He printed up a copy of it for me and I read it over a few times. By the way, Senior Writing Requirements are long papers (thirty page minimum) that every law student has to write before he or she can graduate. After I read and re-read it, outlined it, then read it again, I knew every damn thing anyone could or should know about the subject. I knew the old rule, I knew the current rule, and I had a good idea about how they might change the rule at some point down the road. I knew it all. I had a definitive answer.

So there I am at the next class. I have all my notes in front of me and I am set to give him the best answer he's ever heard. All my friends are riding me before class: "Are you ready, Reppas? Are you ready?" I wasn't bothered by their attempts to frighten me, because they didn't know that I had the perfect answers for any question that the prof might give me on this subject. So anyway, class starts, and the prof is talking about something completely different from where he left off. And he never, ever went back over that subject again. Oh man, did I get hoodwinked. All that work for nothing. Well, I guess the joke was on me.

In case you're curious, here's the short answer is to the

aforementioned question: according to the Florida Bar Rule 4-8.4, "a lawyer shall not: engage in sexual conduct with a client that exploits the lawyer-client relationship." That's it. You can't do it. The reason for this is that you are in a position of power over your client and it would not be right for you to exploit them by using that power to get them into bed. However, if you were sleeping with them before they became your client, you probably will not get into trouble for continuing that relationship. But, I'm sure, if you lose their case they'll probably sue you and throw in the fact that you were also taking advantage of them vy violating Rule 4-8.4.

My recommendation: win the case!

53

Failing The Bar

The Bar Examination is the final test of your knowledge of the law (or at least what you learned of it in school). Honestly, your journey from "A" to "B" does not end at graduation. You still have to pass your state's Bar exam in order to be licensed to practice law. In Florida, the Bar Exam is a three-day test. The first two days test on Federal and State law. The last day is an ethics test.

Anyway, a friend of mine whom we will call "Jason,"[46] graduated two years ahead of me, took a Bar review class, (allegedly) studied hard, but failed.

I'm sure that there were many probable causes for his failure. Let's start with the most obvious one: Jason was a major, and I mean *major* slacker. He skipped class like it didn't matter, and he never studied except for the week before exams. I'm pretty sure that he graduated at the very bottom of his class.

---

46 I'm calling him "Jason" not because that is his name, that would be far too obvious. So let's just agree that I gave him that name because I have to call him something and this name came to me, completely at random, when I needed to give a name to this completely ficticious person..

There's a good chance he didn't study hard enough in the Bar prep class, however, considering how poorly he did in law school, I think it would take him three years to prepare for the exam regardless, as in going back to law school and actually studying this time. Suffice it to say that it didn't shock anyone to hear that he failed. The shock would have come if he passed.

You might be wondering, "How hard do you have to study for the Bar?" You graduate in May and the Bar exam is in July, so that's a lot of time. And you just got out of three years of studying. How hard can this test possibly be? Surely, if I did well in Law School I shouldn't have to study that much, right?

Wrong.

Here's the recommended schedule: in the two months you have to take the Bar Review classes, you need to study for ten hours a day for the first month, and eleven hours a day in the second month, including weekends. During that time, you need to write about fifty practice essays and review two thousand multiple choice questions by taking timed exams and reviewing each question and answer.

So how was my friend doing now that he had to take the exam again?

Not well at all.

Since he couldn't find a job at a law firm anywhere, even to clerk (remember he graduated at the bottom of the class and just failed the Bar), he had to get a job to pay for his $275,000 in student loans. That's no chump change.

He said he was going to declare bankruptcy and just write the debt off, but the bankruptcy lawyer he consulted told him that he could not and that, one way or the other, he had to repay all of it.

I don't know how much it came out per month, but for argument's sake, let's say $2,000 a month. That meant $24,000 a year. So if you start out making $40K a year, you really have $26K. Not good. That would barely cover rent and food. Forget about how long it would take to repay the loan once you add in all the interest. Just know that you'd likely pay until you die.

So, "Jason" was now working as a waiter at some beach bar. He had to sell his car and a lot of his stuff to make ends meet, and he moved into a tiny crap apartment two blocks away from his job with some other waiters who needed a roommate. He told me that he planned to take the Bar again, and again, and again, until he passed. I wished him the best, but there was really nothing I could feel sorry about for him. When you slack that much, you dig your own grave.

VOICE FROM THE FUTURE: It took "Jason" eight (8) years to get admitted to the Bar. I had already been practicing for over five years and was a junior partner in a large firm before he even got his ticket. What a waste! Point "B," people… get to point "B."

54

Law Review

It is without question that the most important and impressive extracurricular activity in Law School is to be on Law Review. The Law Review is a book published by the school's Law Review team (most publish once or twice a year). The book (or "journal" as it called in many schools) includes academic articles written by professors, judges and lawyers on various legal subjects (one in twenty articles, or so, are authored by students). The articles comment on the current state of any particular law, predict where the law is going, or just argue why the law is wrong and why and how it must change. Just as it is an honor to make the Law Review team, it is an honor to be published on Law Review. Very prestigious for all involved and a prerequisite for any professor seeking tenure.

The moment I made Law Review, I actually felt successful. I felt more confident in myself and my abilities as a law student.

I felt as if I had succeeded in Law School. Believe it or not, I felt smarter when I heard that I made the team! And everyone around me suddenly saw me in the same, rosy light. Why? Well, here are some words commonly used to describe a student on Law Review: sharp; intellect; tenacious; high achiever; driven; dedicated; top 5%; and "a rising legal star."

Why all the buzz? Because it is universally accepted that Law Review is comprised of the best of the best in Law School. It is the goal of every student (whether they admit it or not) to do well enough in Law School to make the team and it is the goal of every professor and judge to publish on Law Review. In short, Law Review is the ultimate addition to your resume. Let me put it this way:

Student #1: "I graduated in the top 25% of my Law School class!"

Interviewer: "That's nice."

Student #2: "I graduated in the top 25% of my Law School class, and received 4 Book Awards for being the best student in the class!"

Interviewer: "How nice."

Student #3: "I graduated in the top 25% of my Law School class, and received 4 Book Awards for being the best student in the class, and was on the Mock Trial Team!"

Interviewer: (yawning) "Yes, yes. Very nice."

Law Review

Student #4: "I made Law Review."

Interviewer: "You're hired!"

Okay, you get the point. So let's fast forward. You made the team. Now what do you actually do as a member?

Well, it will not be that glorious of a job for the first-year member (or second-year member who does not make it onto the Board to become one of the elite "board members"). There is an important distinction between a board and non-board member of the Law Review. A board member is a Three-L who has already served a full year as a regular member (during their second year) and was voted by their Law Review peers to a board position. Board members (Editor-In-Chief, Assistant Editor-In-Chief, Articles Editor, etc.) are the true leaders of the team. These are the ones who read all the articles submitted by judges and lawyers and decide which to publish. These are the men and women who run the whole operation.

Naturally this creates a hierarchy within the Law Review itself which could be described as a defacto caste system with board members on top of the pyramid and the non-board members in the row beneath. But once your on Law Review, you discover that it is less of a competition against your fellow members and more of a team effort to get out the best publication that you can.

As to the general members, you should count on doing four things only; all grunt work. And pay careful attention here because you will be spending 30-40 hours a week doing these four things:

(1) Cite checking articles that the Review will be publishing. This means that you will have to track down every book and article referenced by the author you are assigned to. It all depends

on the size of the team and the number of articles in queue to be published, but you will invariably be assigned the task of going to the law library (and often times to other libraries when non-legal sources are referenced) to find each and every book cited by the author, to hunt for the exact page, section, and line that the author cited, and to verify that the line was actually quoted correctly and that the quote means what the author actually said it does. This part of the job is tedious and time consuming.

(2) Make sure that every citation is correctly cited. Meaning that you have to be absolutely, 100% sure that the Bluebook citation is correct. I wrote about citations and the Bluebook exam early on in this book, but trust me, it is difficult when you have so many different sources that need to be perfectly accurate. Again, it takes time.

(3) You have to put in "office hours" every week (usually at least 5 hours), where you will man the phone, ensure that mail is distributed to every member in their "in boxes," and do whatever other secretarial work is required.

(4) Expect at least 30-40 hours of extracurricular time to be put in, week after week, on this job. Yes, that means, 30-40 hours on top of the normal time that you have to put in for all your other classes.

I suspect that number (4) will shock you the most, as it did me. Here were my initial thoughts: "How on earth can I work in a full-time job on top of the double-full time job I have already? All I did was complain about how little time I had just keeping up with all my classes, now I was going to add 30-40 hours into that mix?"

If you get the invitation, then yes, you add in that time. You do what you need to do to keep your grades up to where they need to be and you get the work done. You get it done in the best possible way you can; the highest quality work you can muster. It is that important.

Prospective employers want to hire Law Review members because they know how hard they are capable of working and they know that the end product is top quality work. They predict that you will be able to handle the stress of the job and the hours you will be required to work, because you already demonstrated your ability to do so. Jobs in the big firms and judicial clerkships all go to Law Review members. There are, of course, exceptions to the rule, but Law Review is the rule.

I have heard, but I cannot confirm, that one added benefit to being a member is that you have access to "Law Review Member's Only Outlines" for all your classes.

What?

Is that true?

I have no idea.

55

A Brief Musical Interlude

Law School: The Musical,
Scene 12: "Law Review"

This scene opens with the main character walking up to the door of the Law Review Office. There is a large sign on the door that reads "Law Review" (in black ink) and "Members Only" (in red ink). He has never before entered this room and he is understandably a little nervous. He knows he has to make his debut with confidence, so he pauses at the door to prepare himself.

As he pauses, he notices a tiny sign on the corner of the door that is barely visible, but reads: "Welcome, New Members." He is hoping to have the kind of entrance that would befit a great hero in an old Western movie. The kind where the main character swings open the door and everyone in the room stops whatever they're doing and stares at him with envy and awe. Yes, that is exactly the kind of entrance he wants. He smiles as he pictures this, then grabs the handle and pushes the door open with great strength.

Had he been paying more attention he would have noticed through the glass partition next to the door that the Editor-in-Chief of the Law Review was standing directly behind the door he was now swinging violently open. It is not, exactly, the dramatic entrance he was hoping for, but nonetheless, it was indeed dramatic.

After he apologizes and offers to bring ice for the bruising Editor, main character is told to join all the other new members for their orientation seminar. He takes a seat in the back of the office, embarrassed and perfectly uncomfortable in his chair. After a few minutes the Editor calls everyone's attention and begins her speech. For the duration of her speech she is rubbing her upper arm and doing her very best not to look at the main character.

She stands in front of a large desk with her name etched in a finely carved plate with the words "Law Review Editor-in-Chief," proudly lying underneath. The six members of the Board ominously stand behind her, each memorizing her every word as if it were Gospel. Her disciples diligently pass out Bluebook help sheets as she explains each new member's duties, discusses what their writing assignments are, and assigns them each five hours of office duty per week. She tells them how demanding their work will be, and how they must meet every deadline given to them by the Board. Everything is handled in a very impersonal, matter-of-fact manner.

When her speech ends, another member of the Board assumes her position and addresses the new members. Music fills our ears as the entire Board join him in the opening chorus.

A Brief Musical Interlude

Chorus:
(entire Board)

Welcome to Law Review
So glad you're here
Hope you enjoy
The time you'll serve here

Congratulations
You're a cut above the rest
Welcome to the Club
You rank with the best

Verse 1:
(Board
member #1)

We all know that everybody hates us
They think we're arrogant and pompous
But that's only because they're not on Law Review
Get used to their being jealous

We're the creme de la creme
We're the leaders in this school
And now that you're one of us
You're a winner too

(Board
member #2)

I know I never spoke to you
Before you made the team
But I didn't know how smart you were
Now I regard you with great esteem

You're a member of the Law Review
No longer a simple knave
You're an overnight success story
You became a "somebody" in a single day

Chorus:
(entire
Board)

Welcome to Law Review
So glad you're here

Hope you enjoy
The time you'll serve here
Congratulations
You're a cut above the rest
Welcome to the Club
You rank with the best

Verse 2:
(Board
member #3)

All the best judges and scholars
Were on Law Review in their time
You now have instant credibility
As an academic giant with a great mind

You can write better than anyone
Your citations can never be beat
Your intelligence is greater than ninety-five percent
What you've accomplished is no little feat

(Board
member #4)

Be proud of your new stature
Stand tall above the rest
Now that you're on Law Review
Remind everyone why we're the best

And as you pass by lower students
Carry yourself with your chin up high
Be aloof, be arrogant, be superior
Act as if they don't exist and walk right by

Chorus
& Outro
(entire
Board)

Welcome to Law Review
So glad you're here
Hope you enjoy
he time you'll serve here

A Brief Musical Interlude

Congratulations
You're a cut above the rest
Welcome to the Club
You rank with the best

Main character, along with all the other new members, exchanges friendly handshakes with the members of the Board. In spite of the fact that he injured the Editor-in-Chief, she smiles at him and welcomes him on board.

END NOTES:

The "Bluebook" is a manual used in the legal profession as a uniform way of citing cases, books, articles, etc., in a legal document. The Bluebook sets out the format that writers need to follow so that everyone is doing it the same way. If you want a copy just go to your local Law School bookstore and ask for it by name: The Bluebook, A Uniform System of Citation. The copy that I am using is the Sixteenth Edition.

56

Summary of Three-L

My time in my third year of Law School was dominated by Law Revue and the Immigration Clinic. Even though I made the International Moot Court team, I was so overwhelmed with work in the other groups, that I had to drop out for lack of time. I certainly wanted to be lead chair and argue for my school team against a rival school, but I had no time to prepare and give it the serious effort it required.

Law Revue was the same work-your-butt-off experience that I described previously in this book. The Immigration Clinic was a great experience as well. You may recall early in this book that I stated my pre-law school expectation was to be a practicing immigration attorney. Therefore, it should come as no surprise to you that I applied for and made the Immigration Clinic team at my law school. Because I had taken several immigration law classes and because of my background in international law this was a field that really came easy to me. The clinic was exactly what one would expect – students working for real people who needed their help. I was assigned two cases throughout the year (which was a lot, most students only work on one) and I can tell you that I actually tried two petitions for asylum during my time. Real people. Real cast. Real judge. The real deal.

The cases I tried were very difficult, factually, to prove. Both involved foreigners that claimed that they were tortured by foreign governments and both petitioners claimed that if they were returned to their home country they would be killed.

In both cases, the attorney for the government was a well-seasoned counselor and had at his/her disposal a plethora of statistics and details regarding each of the countries, their governments, the leaders of same and the military and/or the "rebels" that my clients claimed were their tormentors. The details that the government attorneys had at their disposal were incredible, because they had access to the vast, government databases with information about every country in the world. All their political leaders, all their military leaders, everything. Let me make up a hypo for you here to see what I mean.

If your client testifies that "on January 12, 1994, I was attacked in Guatemala City and threated to be shot dead by Omar de la Paca," the government attorney would be able to track down General Paca and for starters would know if this was the type of thing he did to his opponents. He/she might find out that the good general was actually at a peace conference in Helsinki, sponsored by the UN, rather than in Guatemala City beating up your client on that day. Or he/she might find out that Paca never used guns to kill anyone because his weapon of choice was a corkscrew. You get the point.

Because of this clear disadvantage, you have to thoroughly,

I mean thoroughly, research your client's story. The foreign government, the players, the torture methods, everything. And this is about as real as it gets because this is a real client with his/ her future in your hands. If you lose and your client gets deported, they will likely be killed by the same general they just tried to throw under the bus in the US.

I recall one trial in particular that took seven hours for me to put on my case, and my professor gave me the highest praise after my closing argument because not one of the government attorney's objections were sustained by the judge.

Hard work and a lot of stress.

And the results? Well I won on the first case (applause, applause, applause – take a bow and start the "I'd like to thank all the little people who helped me along the way" speech), but I lost the second case. I am proud to note, however, that the record that I preserved during the trial was clear and detailed enough so that the Immigration Clinic students that appealed that ruling the following year were actually successful and the appellate court granted my former client asylum after all.

Other than these team sports, the actual law classes I took were really no different from those in the first or second year other than being conceptually easier. I state this because once you eliminate the harshness of the "Superior Professors," you really find that the teachers just want to get through the material and that the students are a lot more receptive to what it takes to get through the class. So in short summary, everything was a bit easier. Even the stress over the ongoing battles for grades and outlines which lead to fights, melt downs and drama, were, to me at least, less important than in the previous years. They were predictable now and nothing to be overly concerned about.

My mantra for year three was this: "Work hard. Work harder. You're coming into the home stretch!"

57

A Brief Musical Interlude

Law School: The Musical,
Scene 14: "Adieu To Law School,
To Law School, Adieu"

It's 5:16 on a sunny afternoon. The first day it hasn't rained in three years. It is also the last day of exams. Main character exits the exam room triumphantly. Thrilled, not as much with how well he did on his exam, but rather that it was the last one he would take at Law School. As he enters the main area of the campus, he notices four friends basking in the sunlight, laughing and congratulating themselves on finally taking their last Law School exam. The four are the exact same students he met three years ago at the first day of Orientation. They have all grown a bit apart over the last three years, however, on this day it was Fated that they would find each other to bring closure to their three years at law school. As the main character sees them and approaches, he notices that they all are drinking champagne. When they realize he is joining them, they start applauding and cheering him. The celebration has begun because their lives as Law Students is finally over. As they laugh and reflect on their three years together, a recurring theme of their conversation is how none of them can believe how fast their three years together went by. Music then fills the audience's ears as each of them begin telling the others exactly what they will be doing upon graduation.

Main Character:	To be honest, I'm not sure exactly where I'll be After I get this well-earned degree Maybe I'll start practicing . . . but, then again Maybe I'll go for an LL.M. My first goal, however, is to pass the Bar exam After that, Fate chooses where my feet will finally land
Charlie: (jock)	I always thought I'd work for the State Putting scumbags away for their crimes I never dreamed that they'd treat me this way I applied for the job and was denied
	Those Bastards! Don't worry, I'll exact my revenge I'll become the best Defense Attorney in the land I'll keep out as many thieves and murderers as I can I'll do whatever it takes to get back at them
	And I'll make money, more than they could have paid I'll make them regret their decision each and every day

A Brief Musical Interlude

Lisa:
(quasi-
intellect)

Well, on a brighter note, I got the job I was promised
(I start at Daddy's old firm right after grad
They're starting me out at ninety-five
Not counting bonuses… not too bad

Yea, my life is set, things look real good
Thank God I didn't have to try harder
My Daddy got me the interview and I got the job
When I started dating a senior partner

And after the Bar, I'm off to Europe
Spend a couple of months in Spain, Italy, and France
As a graduation gift, Daddy's paying for it all
And he's buying me a brand new Jag

Chorus:
(all
students)

Onward and upward as we say adieu
Our lives as mere students will be over soon
We'll be attorneys! Everyone say it with pride!
No longer will we have to struggle to get by

We'll be out there in the real world at last
No more hypotheticals, no more exams to pass

We'll have real clients with real money
We'll finally get to practice and never have to study

It's our time now, pre-season is finally done
Let's win the big game and show 'em whose number one
Never before have we spoken words so true
Adieu to Law School, to Law School adieu

Law School: How to Get In, Get Through, and Get Practicing

Jason: I have no idea what I'll be doing
(dead-head) When I get out of this place
           I think I'll take the Bar next year
           I need to relax . . . get some space
           I think I'll just take a job as a waiter, part time
           Or something fun like that
           'Cause once I have that degree in hand
           I never have to look back

           The world will be my oyster
           Offers will come pouring in
           I'll pay off my loans in five years max
           And then I'll really start livin'

Sheri: Well I'm very happy to tell you all
(liberal) That I got the job of my dreams
           After passing the Bar I'll start at thirty-two grand
           Working at Legal Services of Miami

           I get to work with the poor
           The impoverished, the abused
           I get to work pro bono
           And get a little salary too

           It's exactly what I wanted
           Helping out those unfortunates in the community
           I don't care how much they pay me
           My goal is piece of mind, not stocks and securities

Chorus Repeat & Outro

A Brief Musical Interlude

The scene ends with each student hugging the other in a final congratulatory embrace. They acknowledge that this will be the last time they will see each other on campus, and they promise to introduce all their parents to each other at graduation the following week. For the Main Character it is a very anticlimactic ending. Saying goodbye to friends can never be a happy occasion. He wonders when he'll see his friends in the future, perhaps it will be in court . . . on opposing sides, perhaps?

> *If that is what is Fated, then so it shall be*
> *For in law all advocates must act as adversaries*
> *Strive mightily and battle with honor to the end*
> *But return home and eat and drink as friends*

END NOTES:

"Pro bono"is a term used by lawyers to say simply that they are providing a service without charging the client any money.

The last four lines of this scene are a play on the Shakespeare lines: "And do as adversaries do in law - Strive mightily, but eat and drink as friends." William Shakespeare, The Taming of the Shrew, Act I, Scene II.

58

Graduation

Well here you are, finally, one step closer to reaching Point "B." Now you're finished with all of your classes, all of the grades are in and the diplomas, caps and gowns, and celebration parties are coming your way. Some of you may be burning text books and/or telling off all of your professors for their past crimes against you and/or going on a three-week bender, but most of you are focused on getting a job and starting to earn some money to pay for all of your debts.

I hope that you will be successful in securing some kind of law clerk job, but if you didn't then I presume that most of you will be looking for a job somewhere, anywhere, again to start paying off the student loans that are piled up in the graduation gift box, ready for you to open the second you get home.

I also presume that a lot of you will be updating your social network pages to let everyone know that you have a new and exciting acronym after your name: "J.D." Congratulations on that.

Finally there will be a few of you who will be taking a nice vacation to celebrate and reward yourselves. Perhaps to Europe or Belize #livingthedream. Hey, I feel like a song!

59

A Brief Musical Interlude

Law School: The Musical, Scene 14: "Graduation"

This scene opens in a well-lit theater on an extraordinary summer morning. A long, wooden, five-foot high stand has been erected in the center of the stage; upon which sits a large podium and a number of very posh chairs. Rows of students wearing long, black robes with frizzy, gold tassels hanging from square, black hats fill the area directly between the main stage and the remainder of the audience. The theater is packed with hundreds of friends and family who are there in celebration of this great day.

As the students laugh and joke amongst themselves, a line of ladies and gentlemen in ornamented, multi-colored robes walk confidently to the stage and take their seats in the cushioned chairs. Main Character is the last person in this line. The students silence themselves as the first of these robed individuals approaches the podium and begins to speak. "Congratulations to our graduating

Law School Class!" he says with a deep and proud tone in his voice. The entire group of students begin cheering and applauding; the audience then follows suit. When the applause dies down the speaker announces to the crowd that he is the Dean of the Law School, and that it is his distinct honor to be the first to congratulate the graduates on their incredible achievement. Again, the applause overtakes him.

After a few seconds, he continues by telling them how he is the luckiest man in the world to have the job he does. That he is very proud of their achievements. That he is confident they will succeed and make valuable contributions to society. And that these graduates will make their alma mater proud. The speech continues in this manner as the Dean regales the captive audience with semi-humorous anecdotes of his experiences with a few members of the graduating class. After he finishes his speech, he calls for the Valedictorian to address his peers and the audience.

Main character rises from his cushioned seat, shakes hands with the Dean and, with a huge smile on his face walks to the podium. He is honored to address his class on this day, and he is comforted to finally have closure on his three years at Law School. The students and audience applaud him as he prepares to speak. He stands silently at the podium, nodding his head in appreciation of the honor bestowed upon him. He has been waiting a long time for the audience to hear his words, and he is thrilled to finally deliver them. Soft music gently fills our ears as his song-like speech is begun.

A Brief Musical Interlude

Welcome family, welcome friends
Welcome to our golden end
The struggle that three years ago we began
Has finally come to this rewarding end

We lived on the concept of deferred gratification
And our reward is finally realized through this graduation
So with great elation I offer you well earned congratulations
Be proud of your achievement, you deserve the adoration

Today many of your parent's dreams have come true
Your families are proud, and I know that you are too
Be proud! What you've accomplished was not done with ease
You've earned the right to call yourselves "Attorneys"

But this is only one step forward in your life, it's true
You still have years and years of journeying left to do
The road you'll travel will be both rocky and smooth
You won't finish unscathed, but I hope your wounds are few

So now go fight for your clients, fight and fight and fight
Ensure that no one is denied their fundamental rights
Now no one will dare kick you down the stairs of life
Without paying for it for the rest of their life

The applause from the audience fills our ears as the curtain
 falls and our musical comes to an end.

END NOTES:

The theme of the quatrain regarding not kicking an attorney down a flight of stairs, was an adaptation of the proverb: "Kick an attorney downstairs and he'll stick it to you for life." Rosalind Fergusson, The Facts On File, Dictionary of Proverbs, 1983.

"The first thing we do, let's kill all the lawyers." William Shakespeare, King Henry VI - Second Part, Act IV, Scene II.

60

Studying for, Taking and Passing the Bar Examination

I'm going to make this very simple and very clear for you. I'm not going to repeat myself. I was very nice by applauding you for graduating from law school. Hurray. You are a "JD." How nice. I don't know many things that are more embarrassing, however, than to have that acronym follow your name without being accompanied by an actual license to practice law.

Should you choose put that "JD" acronym at the end of your name on your resume, business card or personal letterhead without actually having passed that actual Bar examination, then you will, invariably, put yourself in a position where someone will read the acronym and ask you "What is that?" Here's how that exchange will go:

"'JD' is for Juris Doctor, my law degree."

Which will invite the next question: "Oh, I didn't know you were a lawyer?" The answer to which you will require you to explain why you were able to get through Law School and graduate, but not able to pass the Bar examination. Talk about embarrassing.

All that being said, the advice I sincerely offer to you here I hope you follow. STUDY FOR THE BAR EXAMINATION! I don't care how well you did in law school. I don't care if you were top of your class. I don't care how confident you are in your abilities to pass the bar examination. What it will take for you to pass the bar examination is one simple thing: hard work.

For me, it was fourteen-hour days, six days a week, for two and a half months. I did take off Sunday, to spend time with my significant other, and to relax a bit. But my dedication was complete. I studied as hard as possible doing every practice test, study revue, flash cards, outlines on the wall, crib notes/element charts, and listening to audio books from various professors on the core exam subjects. I studied as hard as I could and pushed myself as hard as I could. By doing this, I am very proud to say that I passed the Bar examination on my first attempt. I did very well, in fact. Follow this simple recipe and you should too. No shortcuts!

I have seen many examples of students who did not pass the Bar examination on the first, second, or even sixth try. Trust me, give it one hundred and ten percent the very first time. Make "one and done," your personal mantra.

The following sad story retells the tale of a JD who could not pass the bar examination. Learn from it.

61

One Last Musical Interlude

♪♪♪♪♪♪♪♪♪♪♪♪♪♪♪♪♪♪♪♪♪♪

Law School: The Musical,
Scene 10: "The Non-Practicing Attorney"

This scene opens in a small, dirty pub on the wrong side of town. The pub contains a number of worn tables, worn chairs, and worn patrons. Smoke fills the room. Behind a long wooden bar stand rows and rows of half-empty bottles of gin, vodka, bourbon, whiskey, rum and the standard additions. None of them top shelf brands.

Half hidden behind a bottle of Jack Daniels is a certificate of some sort, mounted to a dark brown piece of wood. It's hard to read. There's a lot of fancy italic script on it with Latin or Greek words hand written in black ink with a golden leaf overlay. Very nice. Beautiful even. It conveys a sense of importance, a sense of seriousness. No one ever looks at it though. No one understands that it is a Juris Doctor degree; a Law School diploma. In this place, nobody would care even if they knew.

A young man lurks behind the bar with a cigarette behind his ear and a second one held tight between his skinny fingers. The ashes, over an inch long, cling to the butt of the cigarette, refusing to fall. He stares off into the distance, ignoring the two drunken patrons who are laughing loudly a few chairs away. His face is unshaven. His hair uncombed. He wears a neon pink shirt that reads "Number 1 Bartender."

His trance is broken by the call for another round by the two drunks. He flicks the ashes of his cigarette onto the floor and carries the remaining butt in his lips. He grabs a bottle of Jack Daniels and quickly pours the patrons their drinks. They eagerly grab the drinks from his hand and swallow them down in one great gulp. They then laugh loudly. The young man stares blankly at them, waiting to see if they want another shot; which they do. After he pours, one patron throws him a ten dollar bill. The young man walks over to an old cash register, taps a few buttons until the till opens, looks around, and then slides the money into his pocket.

He returns the bottle to its place and notices his law degree staring defiantly at him. He can not escape from the memory of his defeat. The bottle before him: Jack Daniels . . . JD, the degree before him: Juris Doctor . . . JD. Then he catches his image in a mirror and is shocked at how haggard he has become; how far he has fallen. Everywhere he turns he is reminded of his failure. He drops his head and falls into another trance his hand still holding the bottle. Music then fills our ears as he begins a soliloquy.

Verse 1:   Graduated four years ago
             Got my JD in hand
             It's worth less than this bottle

One Last Musical Interlude

But it cost me two hundred grand
Graduated at the bottom of the class
Top ninety-nine percent
And I'm pushing drinks at this drunk depot
Trying to pay off my Law School debt

Took the Bar right out of school
Figured I'd pass like all my friends
But, Fate wasn't smiling on me that day
I guess I just have to take it again

Chorus:
(bar
patrons)

We are so sorry for you, non-practicing attorney
You never could have dreamed this would be your end
Why no law firm in town will touch you
We really, really, really, honestly can't comprehend

How could you have known you'd have to study
For the entire three years you were at school
To be able to pass that damn Bar exam
To avoid all the scorn and ridicule

The shame and dishonor make you want to sink
So smoke your smoke, and drink your drink
Everyone around you thinks you're a joke
So just drink and drink and smoke and smoke

Life's not fair, and no one cares
So push away those humiliating stares

Verse 2:

I did have fun for those three years
Parties and parties and friends
But now without any student loan checks
The party has come to an end

I don't make enough to pay my bills
I've hocked pretty much everything I own
My car's been in shop for nearly nine months
And I had to default on my student loans

But I'll saved enough, I promise you this
To take the Bar once more, my friend
It's not my fault that I failed it eight times
I guess I just have to take it again

Chorus Repeat & Outro

Whatever dreams of happiness and success he has are lost as his patrons call for another round. He returns to his miserable reality, knowing full well that he will never escape. The scene ends with the young man lighting another cigarette, pouring himself a shot of whiskey, and swallowing it completely.

62

VOICE FROM THE FUTURE:
How To Get A Job and Why Not To Start Your Own Law Firm Right Out Of School

First and foremost, you need to understand that the entire reason you went to law school was to get a job... as a lawyer. So, now that you are through law school, you need to get that job. Remember, that is Point "B."

This vignette will give you my suggestions on what you need to do to get that lawyer job. As I write this section, I remind you that I am speaking with 20 years of experience in practicing law and in that time I have hired dozens of attorneys (and fired a few as well). After all these years, I know what to look for, I know what is impressive, and I certainly know what is not.

First thing's first: whatever you submit to as part of your application (*e.g.*, resume, writing sample, etc.), make sure it is absolutely in tip top shape! Spell check it. Make sure it is well written and proofed. Spell check it again. Make sure it is absolutely the best presentation you can make. If you error in this department, trust me, the hiring attorney will believe it very likely that if you make mistakes on your job application, you will also make mistakes in the pleadings that you will be preparing for their clients. Do it right, do it once. This is your first impression. Do it right.

Below is a list of practical advice for you. Check these off, one by one, as you complete them.

- Apply to every job opening you can.

- Go to the State Bar Association's job listings page.

- Go to the career placement center at your law school to find job listings.

- Go to online websites for professionals to find job listing (such as LinkedIn, etc.)

- Target a few "dream law firms" where you would love to practice and find a particular partner you want to work with (it's not hard, every law firm has a website identifying all their attorneys and their areas of practice), then start contacting them. Introduce yourself in a nice cover letter. Send them your resume, writing sample, etc. Get their attention. Tell them you want to work for them and tell them why (*e.g.*, because they are so successful, practicing in the area you've dream to practice... flatter them!) And ask for an interview! Ask for it! And if they don't respond, be polite but persistent and keep asking.

- Snail mail your resume to the law firms. Use nice quality paper; trust me, it will make a difference. Of course, if a job listing requests that you only submit your resume via electronic mail, then certainly follow those instructions, but at the very least you should show up at an interview with printed copies of your resume on nice quality paper.

- Be positive and enthusiastic.

- Let your prospective employer know that you will be the perfect soldier in their army. Let them know that you will follow their instructions. Let them know that you will work all the overtime hours they want you to and that you will do the job they ask of you. They want to know that you will give them quality work and bill the hours they need you to bill. A law firm is a business and you are an investment – let them know that you will be a good investment.

- LOOK YOUR BEST FOR AN INTERVIEW. No work-out socks and old, brown shoes. Being unkempt will only insure that you don't get the job. I don't need to be clearer than that. Well, maybe I do: you are not going out dancing at a club, or to a fashion model show, or to a happy hour. You are going to a job interview at a law firm, so dress appropriately.

- Write a "thank you" letter after your interview. Trust me, I appreciate this gesture very much. It shows you took a little extra time to be courteous in acknowledging the time that was spent interviewing you. A hand written note goes a long way in my book.

One very important final note: DO NOT OPEN YOUR OWN LAW FIRM RIGHT AFTER YOU GRADUATE. I know this might seem to be the only possibility for a number of you trying to survive in an over-saturated legal market, but don't. Here's why:

First and foremost, there is a very strong likelihood that you will be doing a disservice to any client you represent. I state this coldly and clearly and I do so because I know of many times in my career where I have litigated against a very young lawyer who hung their own shingle out the day after passing the Bar. Well, it never worked out for their client. Invariably, I crushed each and every one of those opponents in large part because they were unable to follow what I was doing and unable to predict where I was going in my pleadings and at trial. Their lack of knowledge of courtroom procedures invariably surfaced and their inexperience led them to make key mistakes in every case.

I'm not telling you this so I appear to be a fierce litigator (even though I am). Rather, I am doing so in the sincere hopes that I can encourage you to get experience at an existing firm, before you open your own firm. Learn from someone else. Find out how they practice law and how you should practice law. Don't walk into a deposition without the foggiest idea of what the rules are governing a deposition because, you will be embarrassed and your client will likely be taken advantage of as a result.

I know this may be very difficult to hear, especially if you are in a situation where you simply can't get an interview, let alone a job, and you need to start working, but you need to hear it. Perhaps you can work out a co-counsel relationship with an existing lawyer whereby your cases are somehow, supervised by the other attorney (whom you will have to pay, no doubt, a portion of the attorney's fees you are charging your client). Do something to help learn the ropes before you take on any case you are not prepared to handle.

Worst case scenario, look for a job in another city where they are hiring. In my opinion, that is a much wiser choice than starting your career with no experience trying to figure it out on your own and using real people as guinea pigs. Better for you and better for your clients.

Law School teaches you how to think like a lawyer, not how to practice law. They are very, very different things. When you first get out there, you realize fast how much you have to learn.

In all honesty it took me five years of working in a couple of big law firms before I felt comfortable enough to take on a case from its outset through to its conclusion. Of course, everyone is different. I only offer you this advice in the hopes that you don't make any mistakes that can come back to haunt you.

63

Conclusion

I hope this book served you well in your journey from "A" to "B." I certainly wish I would have had it when I started out.

With that said, I look forward to meeting you in court one day. And just so you know, when that day does come, if you let me know you read my book, I will go easy on you (just kidding! I'm going to try and destroy you regardless!).

Sincerely, though, best of luck.

About The Author

 A native of Columbus, Ohio, Mr. Reppas is a graduate of The Ohio State University where he double-majored in Modern Greek Studies and Political Science. Mr. Reppas earned his Juris Doctor degree from St. Thomas University School of Law in Miami, Florida, and his LL.M. degree in International Law from the University of Miami School of Law. Mr. Reppas is a member of the Florida, New York and District of Columbia Bar Associations focusing his practice primarily on Business Law, Music, Art & Entertainment Law, and State, Federal and International litigation. Mr. Reppas is one of the world's foremost legal scholars on Cultural Property and the international debate over the Parthenon Sculptures/Elgin Marbles. Mr. Reppas' academic publications have been cited hundreds of times in leading Law Journals and Books throughout the United States and abroad, and his published theories continue to be referenced by academics and legal scholars throughout the world. Mr. Reppas' works of historical fiction ("Why Don't We Just Sue The British Museum?" and "Ateni Samjak") have fused his trial lawyer skills and knowledge of antiquities law together with his skill as a storyteller to paint compelling pictures of the past. In addition to his law practice and writing, Mr. Reppas is also a lyricist, musician and recording artist. For Mr. Reppas' complete biography and legal areas of practice, please visit: www.REPPASLAW.com.

December --
2020